Financial Freedom for Black Women

A Girl's Guide to Winning With Your Wealth, Career, Business & Retiring Early – With Real Estate, Cryptocurrency, Side Hustles, Stock Market Investing & More!

Brandy Brooks

Disclaimer & Copyright

Dedicated to:

This book is dedicated to my wonderful family, many of whom you'll hear about throughout this book as part of my journey from scarcity to financial freedom. It's also dedicated to my wonderful editor, Jeannie, who has done absolutely everything to ensure this book meets your expectations and beyond. I wish you the greatest luck in the world on your own journey to <u>rightful</u> prosperity and abundance.

Table of Contents

Introduction

"I love to see a young girl go out and grab the world by the lapels. Life's a bitch. You've got to go out and kick ass."

~ Maya Angelou

Financial freedom and financial independence are words we hear in our lives, some more often than not. But, if you're like many Black women, these words sound more like fairytales than realities that we can ever hope to achieve in our lifetime. Why?

Black women have been struggling under the weight of the burden that was placed on their shoulders centuries ago, and we still can't seem to ease the load. Our ancestors worked for nothing under the painful and brutal hands of their enslavers, and even when they achieved freedom, they were still locked out of the system, earning peanuts for back-breaking work. Children were kept out of schools, families out of homes, and because of this, entire generations of Black people have been denied the opportunities to live decent lives. The Civil Rights era saw our great grandparents, grandparents, and parents fight for their place in the room, but every step past the door was met with new obstacles. Schools were letting in our children, but zoning codes were making sure they could only access the bare minimum. We were allowed to get homes, but redlining and financial discrimination ensured we were locked out of the "good" neighborhoods. We stepped foot into companies and got hired, but our pay remained less than our white counterparts and we were told to be grateful we even had a place to work.

With every step forward, we were pulled two steps back. Unfortunately, we are still fighting for our place in the room, and a seat at the table. Even though we face these problems as a race, Black women are getting the short end of the stick compared to our fathers, brothers, and sons; as we still earn less than they do. The decks are stacked against us at home, in the workplace, in our schools, and in our business ventures when we are bold enough to try. Despite our magnificence, resilience, and wherewithal, Black women are measured by standards that set them up for failure. Our heritage, physical features, culture, and personalities are deemed "too much," and we are pushed to conform to the "norm," a code denoted by "white." Everyday, a Black woman is fighting to keep the natural hair on her head, find clothes that cover her distinctive features, and adopt a tone to mask her beautiful voice. As we grow up, we are encouraged to conform to avoid "trouble," but trouble still finds us.

With our identities broken down and stepped on, we spend our time trying to survive, too tired to find a way to thrive. Our success seems out of reach, and with it, our financial freedom.

But, this is not your sign to give up. On the contrary, this is a call to battle - to fight for your place in the room, and at the table. This book is a tool to help you unleash your power to fight for your chance to thrive. To take a step forward, and another, and another. In this book, we will explore how, as Black women, we can step away from our survival era and put in the work to break through to the other end of the wall. Survival is no longer enough. We need financial freedom to thrive.

This book is created to give us a battle plan of sorts, a plan to focus on as we deploy the tools in our arsenal to fight for ourselves. For many Black women, the fight to thrive is not merely a fight against the system around us, but also the beliefs inside us. We need to rise above our own doubts, self-limitations, and conditioned beliefs about financial freedom. We need to change our mindset, and this requires a tremendous change of thought, beliefs, and self-directed actions. This book will focus on the power of mindset in our journey to financial freedom, and explore how other Black women have reaped the benefits of a mindset that screams "Yes! I can! I will! I have!"

7

Our thoughts create our reality. You've probably read this and thought, "what a crock of bs." But have you noticed that the rich always keep getting more and the poor keep getting less? Most of us grew up in households where we were told making money is difficult, so we believe the same. Now, we're cracking under the pressure of just making enough to pay bills, and piling on debt as we try to make the most out of our situations. With this book, the plan is to give you the knowledge and tactics that will get you out of the trenches, and onto the path to financial freedom. We will explore the strategies to help you get out of debt and finally start saving up for a rainy day fund. The plan is to go even further, to help you tap into your power and potential. We will talk about responsible and effective budgeting, creating new income opportunities (side hustles), starting and working on your own business, finding success in your career, and making it up the next rung of the corporate ladder.

However, our focus will not only be on what to do, but also on what NOT to do. Financial freedom is hardly a one-and-done deal, as life will never stop throwing curveballs at us. By looking back at the events of the past couple of years, we realize that creating a cushion for ourselves requires frequently adding a few feathers to keep it nice and comfortable. The 2008 financial recession was a big blow to many of us, and as we fought our way through it, some managed to rise above the fray and settle in for a life of comfort. Unfortunately, the COVID-19 pandemic was like a rug pulled right from under us. While many were already at a disadvantage and the pandemic made it worse, some people found themselves reeling from the consequences of their own actions. We will explore the common pitfalls and traps scattered along the path to financial freedom and the tactics to avoid them or pull yourself out if you get caught.

Finally, this book will explore investment opportunities and how to design the right investment portfolio for you. Investing is a topic that has received immense coverage, but many people fail to realize that we can invest in the wrong thing even though we follow the right advice. Who we are plays a big role in the decisions we make, and financial investments shouldn't be any different. It is counteractive for an anxious person to invest in high-risk ventures, as this can exacerbate their health and wellness. Financial freedom cannot be achieved at the cost of our physical, mental, and emotional wellbeing. And this book strives to help you achieve wealth without sacrificing your health.

My own path to financial freedom has been long and arduous, and I have endured more financial beatings than I ever thought possible. I started working at age 15, mainly to get small change to buy all the things I thought I needed - frequent hair and nail salon visits, trendy clothes, tickets to movie theaters and concerts, and just a little more for my girls' hangouts at the mall. College was not in the cards for me, so I never set any money aside. I made it, I spent it. My brutal wake-up call came at age 18 when my mother got another child (hi Justin!). Things got serious fast. My bank account was hovering just over the $2 mark, and my mother was scrambling to keep us fed. It was then that I realized how much of a burden I had been. I was still working a minimum wage job, but my circumstances had severely shifted. I needed to do something, and fast! Between being a nanny to my brother, a cashier, and a waitress at a nightclub, we were still barely getting by. I worked, scrimped, and fought tooth and nail for my brother, and I finally managed to get into community college.

It's been 20 years since I first got my first paycheck, and seven years since I was finally able to review my finances without first sending a prayer up high. Justin is finally getting into college, and I am happy to say that he doesn't need to take out a loan to get an education - my efforts paid off! But he still has to get a job, not to survive, but to help him see the value of starting early.

Through years of hard work, numerous books and blogs later, I got my happy ending. My trial and error paid off, and I have grown wiser in my endeavors. This book is a culmination of everything that worked for me along the way and the lessons I learned from my many mistakes. My goal is to help Black women like myself approach financial freedom from a position of self-empowerment and conscious living. Finances shouldn't be a topic we dread, but a challenge we embrace and fight to overcome. Budgeting, investing, and putting in extra effort are not activities that draw us away from our happiness, but are tools and techniques that push us closer to the individual we want to be.

We will highlight how grit and the courage to dream propelled Black women in history to become the heroes we need, showing us that no matter what, we do have the choice to make our lives not only comfortable, but worth it. Fannie Lou Hamer, Oprah Winfrey, Michelle Obama, Maggie Lena Walker, and Lilla St. John are just some of the women who proved that stereotypes are a bunch of hogwash, and that no matter what we face, we do have the power to implement change, to raise ourselves and our communities to greater heights - to show our mothers, sisters, and daughters that success is the norm, not the outlier. To fight against the poverty mindset and embrace the growth and abundance mindset.

We will walk the path to financial freedom together, and I will show you how to make it through the darkness and into the light. The techniques in this book are yours to employ as you see fit, but I can promise you that by embracing the concepts and applying them in your life, you will step closer and closer to the joys of financial freedom and independence - and the person you deserve to be.

Here, take my hand, and let's jump into the deep end together. I promise you, I'll be holding your hand every chapter along the way until we make it to the very end. 1…2…3… Let's begin!

Chapter 1 - Why Black Women MUST Become Financially Free

"The most common way people give up their power is by thinking they don't have any."

~ Alice Walker

The History that Bled Into The Present

Black History in America is filled with stories of pain, tragedy, and unrelenting oppression. Our heroes pushed through insurmountable adversity to have their voices heard, but years later, we are still fighting the war. Every step we took forward was received as a threat and we were pushed back. I am using the past tense, but as Black Women, we all know that this is still pretty much what we go through every single day. Slavery took away our freedom to choose, and we were subjected to brutal punishment for daring to break away from the mold. For the white man, slavery was just a way of milking productivity from Black men, women, and children - the cost of doing business. When tobacco ceased to be as productive

13

because of the depleted soil nutrients, the slave trade diminished, but the trade regained momentum once cotton became a high-demand commodity[1]. Our pain, discomfort, and humanity didn't exist. We were only as valuable as the labor we provided, and none of the proceeds made its way to us. The slaves who worked without causing trouble were considered role models to be emulated by the "troublesome" slaves who were quickly disposed of if they were deemed more trouble than they were worth.

When we finally attained our freedom, they found new ways to keep us in gilded cages. Slaves were declared free in America, but they were left at the mercy of the same people who had enslaved them[2]. Angry and resentful that they had lost the Civil War, the southern whites quickly found new ways to keep our ancestors down - by passing laws that made it impossible for Black men, women, and children to rise above the fray. The effects of these laws are still felt today in our residences, education system, workplaces, and finances.

In 1933, the Home Owners' Loan Corporation (HOLC), a government-sponsored organization, needed to establish criteria for citizens to get access to low-interest mortgages in the wake of the Great Depression. The answer - was a color-coded mapping system for zoning neighborhoods based on their perceived financial health[3]. Neighborhoods marked green were determined to be "Best," those marked blue meant they were "Still Desirable," those marked yellow were "Definitely Declining," and those marked red were "Hazardous." While some experts argue that this system was created purely from an economic aspect and was not racially motivated, its implementation had devastating effects on Black communities. The practice was dubbed "redlining," and it has stretched its tendrils into the very fabric of homeownership discrimination in America. Black communities were already marginalized and financially downtrodden, but the Great Depression dealt them an even bigger blow. Black men and women were the first to lose their jobs, their unemployment rate was three times higher compared to white people, and they were less likely to receive government financial aid, and if they did, they received substantially less than their white counterparts[4]. Is it surprising then that most Black neighborhoods ended up in the HOLC's red zones? The obvious answer is no!

Our homes were smack dab in the middle of the red zones, and any homes close to these boundaries were automatically designated yellow. With this lending system in place, a disproportionate number of our parents, grandparents, and great-grandparents were deemed ineligible to access the cheap government-sponsored mortgages. When we did have money to buy houses, realtors made sure we never saw the listings in the desirable green and blue zones, as our presence would "disrupt" the "stability" of our neighborhoods. While redlining was outlawed in 1968, we are still living in a community where the color of our skin devalues the price of our homes. In 2021, Californian couple Paul Austin and his wife Tenisha Tate Austin wanted to put their house on the market, so they called in an appraiser. They bought the home for $889,000 in 2016, and had $400,000 worth of renovations done, adding 1000 sq ft to the home. In 2021, they were told their house was only worth $989,000. Shocked, the Tates decided to run an experiment. They called in another appraiser, and this time they had a white friend play the role of the homeowner. You know where this is going, don't you? The home was valued at... drum rolls please... $1,482,000[5]. The Tates, unfortunately, are not an isolated case study. If you have a moment, look up the Abena and Alex Horton story[6]. References can be found at the back of the book.

Our forefathers and civil rights heroes advocated for access to education, firmly believing that educated Black men, women, and children would have a greater chance to lift the community from the murky trenches of poverty and destitution. As we rallied to get our children in schools, segregationist laws made sure we were kept well away from the classrooms with access to sufficient resources. The "separate but equal" rule was a joke, as there was nothing equal about the education Black children were getting in school. Furthermore, schools were subject to the same redlining policy that was placed upon our homes because children were not allowed to attend schools in different zones, a policy that still applies today. Attendance zone boundaries have propagated the inequalities that exist in our education system, locking out Black kids from the resources they need to excel. Black mothers with promising young kids watch helplessly as their children attend schools that are ill-equipped to hone and foster their potential because they cannot afford to move to "better" neighborhoods with "good" schools. Homes lose value if they are located in neighborhoods with "bad" schools, keeping out the very resourceful homeowners whose voices can push for change.

In 2012, Tanya McDowell began serving her five-year sentence. Her crime? "Stealing an education." Tanya had grown up in Bridgeport and knew how lacking the education system was, and how much better it was over in Norwalk. In 2010, homeless and shuffling from shelter to shelter in Bridgeport and Norwalk, Tanya decided to use her friend's address to enroll her son in a Norwalk kindergarten because she knew the district's education system was "better" than Bridgeport's. She was among a dozen other parents who broke the law just to see their children get a shot at success. Of all the parents who did the same thing, Tanya was the only one who faced criminal charges, and a subsequent five-year prison sentence[7]. Fast forward to 2019 and millions of people are watching as Felicity Huffman and husband William H. Macy clasp hands tightly as they walk out of court. After spending $15,000 to get her daughter's SAT scores and college applications doctored so that she can attend the college of her choice, Felicity Huffman got decades in prison, right? Of course not. That would mean this is a fair world. She got 14 days[8], and was released early! I still don't know what is more heartbreaking - that Huffman getting time in prison surprised me, or that I was sure she would get away with it.

If we're not fighting for our right to own good homes or to get a decent education, we are fighting to keep our physical traits AND right to earn an income. For as long as I can remember, my mother's hairline has been shot to hell. She's always worked as a secretary, so she always made sure that her appearance was "acceptable." While working at an Evangelical church, she kept her hair straightened, resorting to harsh chemical treatments and a boatload of products so that no strand was out of place. She carried around hair products, combs, and brushes in her purse, ready to "spruce up" at a moment's notice. When, inevitably, her hair thinned out, she turned to weaves and wigs, making sure that even if they had curls, it wasn't too "wild." So, when I started working at 15, she made sure I learned all the tips and tricks to keeping my hair in place. It didn't matter that I was working at a fast-food restaurant and always had my hair covered. My second job was as a cashier at a department store, and I quickly began emulating my mother. By 18, my hair was falling out. I didn't have the purchasing power to get good products, so the damage was swift and relentless. Like my mother, I quickly embraced weaves and wigs even though my scalp was too sensitive, and braiding left me in pain for days on end.

Thankfully, I cut my hair at 19, and for the next decade, kept it short enough that I could wear wigs without much fuss, and even on days I went without, I was already working in the back office, so my bosses didn't care about the girl with the 'fro. My mother, and many Black women in the nation, have no choice but to jump through hoops just to be deemed "professional." And if we choose not to comply with these arbitrary standards, we pay the price.

In 2010, Chastity Jones interviewed for a position at a call center in Mobile, Alabama. Dressed in a sharp business suit and pumps, she was ready to impress, and impress the interviewer she did. She got the job, but there was a catch - her hair. Jones sat in the interview room and listened as the interviewer told her that the hair on her head - styled in short, natural locs - "violated the company's grooming policy" because they "tend to get messy[9]." When she sued for discrimination, the Alabama federal district court took the company's side, arguing that she had to show that the bias was against a trait that she couldn't change to prove discrimination. In short, since her hairstyle could be changed, she was not discriminated against. In 2016, the 11th Circuit Court of Appeals upheld the decision, and refused to review the case in December 2017. The absurdity of the court's reasoning is appalling to Black women, but it has been our reality for centuries in this country.

Cultural imperialism has plagued our community from the time the white man decided to pluck Black men and women from their homes and ship them as commodities that could be traded, gifted, or used as collateral on debts and obligations. They deemed our religions unworthy and Christianity the "right" religion, so we converted. They looked at the hair on our heads and deemed it "inappropriate," so we adopted harmful practices to conform to their standards. Our music was considered "noise," "violent," "inappropriate," and other derogatory terms until it became profitable for them. When they adopted the music, their sons and daughters were praised for transcending artistic boundaries. We have watched as white women have undergone multiple surgeries to achieve the curves that we were berated for years. And now that the curves are no longer trendy, we are watching as we are once again cast aside as they chase the new beauty standards.

Black culture is beautiful, powerful, and fundamentally unique, and for centuries we've watched helplessly as we were forced to betray our own selves to fit what was considered "normal," which was just the politically correct description for "white." Black women have spent millions of dollars on skin products that promise to lighten their skin. We have put money in the pockets of companies selling hair products not designed for our locs, enduring irreversible damage in the process. Our fashionable expression was dubbed "urban," and appropriated by white designers without credit to the people who dared to be bold enough to step away from the norm. Our sons' and daughters' fashion choices have been slammed and looked down upon for years, but when a white celebrity copies us, it's considered a stamp of approval.

In our financial institutions, Black men and women are finding themselves paying the price for wanting more out of their lives. When the real estate market crashed in 2008, studies uncovered something disturbing about the lending institutions' practices - a majority of the problematic subprime loans had been disbursed to the minority communities[10]. These predatory lending practices are not limited to mortgages. Car dealers are often more than willing to suggest loan options that set us up for failure. We grow up with the lesson that the institution employees know better, so we are more likely to take the advice

21

given by the representative. Unfortunately for many Black men and women, dreams have quickly turned into financial nightmares, resulting in a high rate of defaults, leading to repossessions and foreclosures.

Dare to Be Successful and Happy

I am happier now than I have ever been in my life. Why? Because I see young Black women rising en masse and fighting for their right to be unique. Black-owned hair and beauty companies are giving us the options we didn't have a decade ago, and our children are spared the torture of smelling their hair burning in the kitchen. I had to buy my mother a new stove because I could never stop smelling my hair whenever I drew the short stick and had to cook. Our skin color is now represented on makeup shelves, and we no longer have to look like the ghost of Christmas Eve when we go out. Black content creators are paving the way for our children to find ways to express themselves uniquely and without fear. On social media, we are pushing companies to represent us positively in the media, and fighting for our brothers and sisters who have been the unfortunate victims of the system. We are pushing for change, but it is not enough to just shout at the top of our lungs. We need to fight for the positions that will give us a chance to hear the voices of our daughters, sisters, and mothers, and do something about it.

Growing up, I had no choice but to watch shows where Black people were either cast as criminals or for comedic relief because they were always airing. But it wasn't until I started watching sitcoms with Black cast that I was truly mesmerized by TV. I couldn't believe that they lived in homes that I never imagined Black people could have. The *Fresh Prince of Bel Air* had a mansion where each kid, even the visiting cousin, had their own room. I was in awe. *My Wife and Kids* featured a home with a well-paved basketball court and a hoop with a net whose holes were not ripped. The homes were always clean and meals were served on platters. The beauty of these shows for me was not the jokes or the stories, but the premise that Black people could live like that. I shared a bedroom with my mother until I turned 13 and we moved. When my brother was born, I knew our living arrangements would need restructuring. In the end, we put a divider in my bedroom so that my brother and I could have some semblance of privacy. It worked, but none of us were happy about it. This pushed me to find a better paying job so that we could move to a bigger space.

When I think about why I wanted to be successful, my mind immediately conjures the shows that showed me a different side of Black communities. As a teenager, *Girlfriends* revived my need to get a taste of success. While my motivation was material at first, this morphed into something bigger as I watched my brother grow up. Justin was a very expressive child, and as mom and I worked our butts off to make sure he was well taken care of, I started noticing a pattern. He'd be stressed when we were stressed, and relatively happy when we were doing okay. This realization shifted something inside me. Instead of working just to have money to buy him extra toys, I began thinking of ways to make more money so that I could have time to decompress and just enjoy time with Justin. I hoped that by becoming less strung up I could counter my mom's darker days by shining a little bit of light.

Success for Black women is more than just making more money. Our success is a beacon of hope for the Black community, a message that we can, and are, capable of achieving the levels of success that our ancestors could only dream of. As Black women make strides in each industry, rising from the depths of despair to comfortable living, the next generation of Black women grow up with evidence of Black excellence all around them. In November and December 2021, social media was flooded with videos of Black girls and boys expressing excitement because they had seen cartoon versions of themselves in a Disney movie. *Encanto* is a film that has been hailed for its representation of minority communities, and is proof that representation matters. When we see people who look like us achieving great things, our brains receive the message that we too can do it. As more Black women start businesses, rise up the ranks, create content for the community, and contribute to the community, our children grow up with evidence of success all around them. This is a greater motivating factor than all the speeches and books combined. We are more inclined to believe what we see, and success is no different.

But there's always a caveat. Success should not be pursued at the cost of our own happiness. Black women have always stepped or have been pushed aside to make way for others, and our well-intended sacrifices have seen us reduced into shells of our magnificent selves. Sometimes I imagine how I would have turned out if I had seen my mother's impulsive side more often. She absolutely loves music, and sometimes I would come home from school and find her dancing around in the house, singing and dancing without a care in the world. But these moments were few and far between because she had to work long hours, most of the time on volunteer projects, because saying no when she was asked would see her sidelined at work by the other employees.

If we have the chance to look out for ourselves, we need to take it. Capture these moments and hold tight, making sure that we fight for our emotional and psychological wellbeing. Pushing for success means we will face difficult moments, but we need to make sure that the difficulties don't rob us of our chance to experience the beauty in our lives. As I said before, I am happier now. Black women are working overtime to carve out their spaces in the world, and showing us how to take care of ourselves in the process. Oprah's *Soul Sessions* have opened up our world to the benefits of self-care, given us access to the teachings of renowned leaders, and allowed our role models to share their stories of struggles and triumphs. Other Black creators are giving us access to information on investing, money management, health and wellness, financial wellbeing, and family matters. The world of social media, despite its flaws, has allowed the Black community to reach their audience without relying on media corporations that have locked us out for years. I am happy because when I search for books by Black women on Amazon, I see my sisters' works spanning genres and niches. I am happy because YouTube has Black women sharing information on every imaginable topic, and I feel validated that my interests are not "abnormal."

I am happy that Black women are constantly pushing the boundaries, and I cheer every day for every woman who breaks the mold.

Chapter 2 - The Mindset of Wealthy Black Women

"When I dare to be powerful, to use my strength in the service of my vision, then it becomes less and less important whether I am afraid."

~ Audre Lorde

"Live your truth."

"Be authentic."

"Words of affirmation."

"Mindset. Mindset. Mindset."

In the past year, I have heard these words countless times. Sometimes I get frustrated when someone mentions the word mindset and I'm going through a difficult time, but somehow it always seems to give me the boost I need. First, it redirects my attention from my problems to the person who said it, and second, it reminds me that I need to perform my obligatory checklist - "Is the problem solvable? Yes. Solve it," and "Is the problem solvable? No. Find a way to adapt." This was a lesson I learned, not the hard way, but it definitely wasn't easy either. I'd find myself obsessing over tiny things that I had no time to focus on what I really needed to do. My mom typically worked from 10 am to 4 pm, Monday to Monday. Her days off were unpredictable, and when Justin came along, I initially had to quit working because we couldn't afford help. Within three months, our house was a warzone. We barely had any money for utilities, let alone the three of us. My mom started hoarding coupons, but my teenage pride wouldn't allow me to use them. If I went shopping alone, I would swipe the magic card. The little allowance mom gave me was barely enough to cover the credit card fees, so I got another one. Six months later, I had five cards, and I was thousands in the hole. I kept this hidden from my mother until one day the credit card company called when I was out of the house. When I got back home, my room was turned upside down, and my cards thrown on the floor. Mom was enraged. What followed was an argument that was the mother of all arguments. When our voices were hoarse and energies depleted, mom lay sobbing on the kitchen floor, and I was curled up with Justin in her room, all cried out. Only one part of that entire situation stuck with me - the sight of my usually put-together mother lying on the grimy floor, disheveled, and face swollen. The mood in the house remained somber for a week.

My pride had created chaos where there was a delicate balance. I am grateful for that day because it was the slap in the face I needed. I began seeing my mother as my partner and not just a parent. We were in this fight together, and I had to start pulling my weight.

In November 1903, a Black woman managed to accomplish the unthinkable, opening a Black-owned financial bank. Saint Luke Penny Savings Bank, later The Consolidated Bank and Trust, was the realization of Maggie Lena Walker's dream to have Black people achieve financial independence from their white employers by pooling their resources together. Walker was the daughter of a former slave, and she watched as her mother turned to washing laundry for white folks to support the family after her father's death. Tasked with returning the clothes to their owners, Walker witnessed firsthand the economic disparity between her people and their white employers. She became a teacher, but had to quit because the school prohibited the employment of married women. She joined the Independent Order of St. Luke, working in different roles until she took over as the Grand Secretary 11 years after she first joined. Under her leadership, the organization rose from the brink of bankruptcy and into a financial behemoth for the Black community, and the creation of the first Black-owned bank in the country. Maggie Lena Walker is now remembered as the first Black woman to create and serve as the president of a bank in the United States[11].

On May 7, 1953, a story article ran in *Jet Magazine* titled "Woman Passes N. Y. Stock Exchange Exam." The right side of the article featured a picture of Lilla St. John, a 25-year-old mother of two. The first sentence of the three-sentence article read, "Mrs. Lilla St. John., certified investment counselor with Oppenheimer and Company on Wall Street, became the first Negro woman to pass the New York Stock Exchange examination for financial advisors[12]." She'd sat for the exam after just two months of cramming, a fete previously unheard of. For Black women in the financial sector, these two paved the way for Black girls and women in the country. Despite the discrimination and obstacles pushed into their paths, Walker and Lilla St. John still reached for their dreams, and left a legacy.

In 2020, 91% of Black women who voted in the presidential election cast their vote in favor of Joe Biden[13]. Leading up to the historic election, Black women all over the country - rappers, students, musicians, actresses, politicians, television hosts, and even adult entertainers - flooded our social media timelines with a single purpose in mind: to get as many of us as possible to the polls. We watched as our fellow Black women fought against misinformation and propaganda one tutorial at a time, with Michelle Obama taking the time to teach us how to make sure our mail-in votes would be eligible. We were instructed on how to avoid making mistakes in the mail-in votes, encouraged to get our elderly to the polling stations, and confirm we were registered voters. We showed our strength in our numbers, and following the results of the elections, we are watching as red states have launched fights to suppress our votes. Our right to vote would not have been possible if not for women like Fannie Lou Hamer, who pushed against the voter suppression laws and tactics that were employed to keep us from the polling stations. Voters had to pass literacy tests and pay poll taxes, conditions that meant Black people would be disproportionately ineligible to vote since we were denied education and we had little means to afford the taxes. Hamer, despite the threats, ridicule, arrests, police brutality, and hate she endured, pushed through, mobilizing Black women to rise against the system locking them out. The Voting Rights Act of 1965 was the realization of a dream that had seen countless Black men and women make sacrifices that many of us would deem too extreme. However, we are still fighting for our right to vote, and with Black women like Stacey Abrams, LaTosha Brown, and others working tirelessly against the system, it is in our best interest to give them the support they need.

On February 13, 2022, 29-year-old Erin Jackson cemented her legacy - she became the first Black woman to win a gold medal in the 500-m women's speed skating race at the Beijing Winter Olympics. The first Gold medal in speed skating that America snagged since 1994. She is also the first Black woman to join Team USA as a speed skater[14]. After becoming the first Black female swimmer to win an individual Olympic gold medal during the Rio 2016 Olympics, Simone Manuel said[15]: "I'm super glad that I can be an inspiration to others and hopefully diversify the sport. But at the same time, I would like there to be a day where there are more of us, and it's not 'Simone, the Black swimmer.' The title 'Black swimmer' makes it seem like I'm not supposed to be able to win a gold medal, or I'm not supposed to be able to break records. That's not true because I work just as hard as anybody else, and I love the sport. I want to win just like everybody else."

On July 8, 2021, 14-year-old Zaila Avant-garde became the first African American to win the Scripps National Spelling Bee[16] since the event's advent 90 years ago. Before her, 12-year-old Jamaican Jody-Anne Maxwell was the first non-American to win the contest in 1998. It doesn't matter where we look, Black girls and women are rising above the stereotypes imposed upon them, the limits set by others, to become the best in their chosen fields. Before Venus and Serena Williams was Althea Gibson, the first African American to win the French, Wimbledon, and U.S. Open singles championships[17]. In every field and industry there is a Black woman who dared to dream. To dream of living up to her potential, no matter the cost. Countless Black women have put in the work, striving for the betterment of their families, communities, and themselves. And there are countless more who have resigned to their fate, settling for the crumbs that fall to the ground. They teach our children to color within the lines, to accept that there is not much for them in the world. How many times did you (or do you) hear the words "Black people don't do that" while growing up? How many "jokes" have been made about Black women who dared to defy the limitations of what it means to be "Black"? Fortunately, Black women and girls are constantly daring to shift their realities, rising from the trenches to show the world what they are capable of.

When she was asked what the a-ha moment in her life was, Oprah Winfrey responded that it was the moment she realized that her thoughts controlled her whole life. "If you want your life to be more rewarding, you have to change the way you think," she wrote[18]. In her book, *Becoming*, Michelle Obama writes about how her work in the White House left her little time to focus on herself and her family, resulting in a future version of herself that was far removed from what she had envisioned[19]. She recalled a speech her husband, then her boyfriend, had given in a church. Speaking to the neighborhood group of people grappling with hopelessness and indifference, Barack Obama stated: "You got somewhere by building that better reality, if at first only in your own mind."

Our minds are powerful, but so many of us fail to notice just how powerful. Every action, decision, habit, choice, and behavior is first constructed in our minds before it materializes in our reality. Some of our habits are so automatic that we assume that's just the way it is, but when we look far back, there was a time we were making those decisions consciously. I remember when I first got hired as a cashier in a beauty store. The vast array of products scared me, as I was not sure I would be able to advise the customers on what to use. The manager, a 21-year-old I'll call Marie, would just rattle off the products and isles they were at whenever a customer walked in and asked for help. I was at best an average student, and cramming was not my forte. It took me about five months before I stopped deferring to Marie every few minutes. I didn't even know how good I'd been at it until my mother came to the store one afternoon. I was busy, so I just told her where she'd find what she was looking for. That night, she couldn't stop praising my professionalism and "smartness." Eight months into the job, I was helping Marie fill order slips because I could somehow remember which products were running low and which ones were needed by our bulk customers. In the years I worked at the store, I watched as students who'd been better than me in school quit because the work was too difficult, opting instead to work longer hours at the food joint a couple of blocks away.

34

"Whether you think you can, or think you can't...
you're right." When I first heard this statement, I
dismissed it as another quote by a privileged white
man who didn't understand the struggles of relying on
minimum wage to survive. However, following the
blowout with my mother, I realized that something
had to change. I had to become the hope my mother
had been waiting for, no matter what happened. I went
back to the beauty store, and while Marie had moved
on to better prospects, the owner was willing to take
me back, this time as a manager. The pay was just a
couple of dollars higher than what I'd made as a
cashier, and the workload much heavier. Every penny
I made was spent on Justin's care, while mom covered
bills and utilities. A few months into this arrangement,
I realized I needed to make more money. With few
prospects available, I accepted a job at the same
nightclub my friend was working at. They needed help
from Thursdays to Saturdays because of the influx of
customers, and were willing to pay cash. I jumped at
the chance. I hated the work in the first few weeks,
until a new bartender was hired. Claris was a short
stocky woman in her 40s, and she'd just left her
husband. She took me under her wing almost
immediately, and this is how the idea of going to
college was first planted in my mind.

Claris would talk about her life with ease,
lamenting how she'd given up her chance to go to
school because of love. "Don't be like me, darling.

Make something of yourself." When she'd see me flirting with a patron, she'd find me later and say things like, "Focus on getting your money baby girl," "There's nothing as beautiful as having your own nest egg," and other statements that had me accusing her of being obsessed with money. One night, tired and frazzled because a crush of mine had asked for my number, Claris made her usual statement, and I snapped. "Money doesn't make you happy!" I shouted, immediately apologizing when she just stared at me in shock. Instead of focusing on my apology, she responded, "Then what does?"

I had no answer.

This encounter got buried with my other memories, and it wasn't until years later that I realized how problematic that statement was. Claris had a point. We are all ready to shout, "Money doesn't make you happy," and "Money is the root of all evil." But do we ever sit back and wonder where this belief originated from? Many of my problems were solved once I paid off my credit card debts. When the threat of starvation or homelessness was removed, I was able to focus on getting an education and finding my niche in the world of finance. I know a number of Black women who say the same thing.

When Deepak Chopra took the stage on Oprah's *Super Soul Sessions*, he described our mind's role in creating our reality. When a message is reinforced, over time we start believing it as the truth. These truths become our beliefs, and as we see the events of our world reflect these beliefs, we become more convinced. This cycle rages on, until we consciously decide to break free. For many Black women, any conversation pertaining to finances has been mired in negativity, particularly highlighting the lack of it. My mom was fond of saying, "Money doesn't grow on trees," but she would pay the bills and then spend what was left over on anything that caught her fancy. My grandmother was tightfisted, so much so that she would have me and my cousins living off sandwiches for days over the holidays even though our parents always gave her money to cover our needs. When she passed away, our parents discovered tins filled with cash squirreled away all over the house. At 15, I had picked up my mother's habits, lamenting about how hard it was to make money but blowing it all on random items I never really used. My friends had the same habits, and we'd laugh together when the next "broke" spell hit us.

I look back at this time fondly, but my heart breaks every time I notice young women and girls falling victim to this cycle. When I finally started working on my finances, I became obsessed with the come-up stories of women like me. My internet search history was filled with personal finance stories and interviews of successful women, including Gayle King, Oprah Winfrey, Gabrielle Union, and Shonda Rhimes. I read so much that it all seemed to bleed into each other, and the messages began seeming redundant. While their stories were diverse, there was one aspect that remained constant - their lives changed for the better after they changed their way of thinking.

Every successful Black woman has another Black woman she looks up to, someone who dared to defy their own odds. When I need inspiration in my self-improvement journey, I think of Oprah. How she managed to push through the trauma of her childhood abuse and find a way to thrive in this world even with the deep scars. As more Black girls fight for their place, they look at those who came before them, those who persevered and fought like hell to make their dream a reality. The achievements made by Lilla St. John, Fannie Lou Hamer, and Maggie Lena Walker, were a result of tremendous courage, unparalleled perseverance, and a belief so strong that it transcended every obstacle thrown in their way. We live in a world that still pushes us to the bottom of the ladder, but we are also blessed to be living at a time when Black women embody the courage that changes the world. Oprah was not content with hosting a gossip-riddled show, so she transformed the *Oprah Winfrey Show* into a beacon of hope, a show about healing and fighting to be whole even with scars. This courage to do something new turned her into a powerhouse, an icon for Black women and girls all over the world.

Most of us are not going to be world famous athletes, actors, or activists, but we do have our own sphere of influence. We have the power to change ourselves, our environments, and our communities. By choosing excellence in everything we do, having the courage to delve into the unknown, and believing in our capabilities, we teach our minds to expect nothing but the best. We shift our minds to believe in ourselves, to get used to challenges that make us better, and even if we fail, we can rest assured that we tried. Success looks different to different people, but at the core is the "can do" mindset that drives our thoughts, words, and actions. In essence, "mindset, mindset, mindset" is not an annoying buzzword, but a lighthouse that draws us towards the shores of success.

Chapter 3 - Getting Out of Debt (from Negative to $0)

"It's crazy that I can't imagine the day when I'm not paying. I'm just so used to giving these people money."

~ Heather Pinckney

The Numbers

I couldn't used to imagine a life without some form of debt bearing down my back, and I am not alone. Practically veryone I know is paying for some sort of financing, whether it is their mortgage, student loan, car loan, credit card loan, or a line of credit they took out on their business. When the Institute of International Finance (IIF) released its 2021 report, many financial experts were not really surprised by the amount of debt racked up in the country, especially considering how COVID-19 affected our financial lives. The global debt has reached an all-time high, totaling $296 trillion at the end of June 2021, according to the Institute of International Finance[20]. This is a remarkable $36 trillion jump from the pre-pandemic levels. As experts at the IIF predict, if the current borrowing trends continue, the global debt will surpass $300 trillion. The United States national debt surpassed $30 trillion in early 2022, as the national debt clock shows[21]. I've always been mesmerized by the numbers on the national debt clock, but as I stared at it while working on this book, I was shocked to see that the federal debt to GDP ratio was at 125%. Considering how the pandemic wreaked havoc on the economy, which wasn't that stable anyway, I understood how this came about. But as the pandemic surges on, the federal debt level is just the tip of the iceberg.

As nations ramped up borrowing to mitigate the effects of the virus, its citizens were reeling from its effects - physically, emotionally, psychologically, and financially. Even before the pandemic reared its ugly head, American households were struggling to keep up with the rising costs of necessities. Income has remained relatively the same for most people, but collectively, there has been a 3% reduction in the median income in the past two years. With the cost of living within the same period rising by almost 7%, families had to find a way to pay for food, utilities, medical costs, gas, and fulfill their other obligations. A report by the New York Federal Reserve shows how borrowing rose in 2021, and in the fourth quarter of 2021, the average American household debt was at 15.58 trillion[22], translating to about $155,622 per household. This was a 6.2% increase in borrowing in just a year. This amount spans various forms of borrowing, including student loans, mortgages, credit cards, auto loans, home equity lines of credit, and various household obligations. Mortgages constitute the largest portion of household debt, and in 2021, $4.5 trillion worth of new mortgages were issued, and mortgage balances in the country rose by $258 billion. Mortgage debt, as calculated at the end of December 2021, is now at $10.93 trillion. $181 billion worth of new auto loans were processed in 2021, while overall credit card balances rose by $52 billion. The total outstanding consumer debt totals $4.2 trillion, with credit card debt making up $807 billion. However, while the total credit card balance rose, the balances carried over from month to month actually reduced by about 14% as of September 2021, bringing this balance to $357 billion[23]. Student loan debt in America currently totals $1.75 trillion[24]. In the fourth quarter of 2021, student loan debt increased by $21 billion compared to the fourth quarter of 2020. However, this was an 8% reduction compared to data collected over the past two decades.

The Nuance of Debt

While the median debt statistics may make you believe that we are all sharing the burden of debt equally, the short answer is that we are not. The reasons why we get into debt vary, as do the quality of the debts we manage to receive. The inequalities and discriminations that Black people have had to endure in other sectors has not spared them from being on the losing side of financial borrowing. 68-year-old Sherry Long was just 10-years-old when she watched as her mother was accused of not paying her water bill after she paid $300 in cash at the municipal council office in Rawlings, Wyoming. As Sherry watched her mom cry after being accused of lying, and having to live in debt to get the water turned on, she became weary of financial institutions[25]. Unfortunately, Sherry's story is not an anomaly. *Washington Post* columnist Michelle Singletary recalled one time when her grandmother got a call from an auto loan representative, telling her that she had missed one of her monthly payments. Michelle's grandmother, Big Mama, was a stickler for making payments early, she never missed a payment, and she recorded every single transaction she made. As the representative listened on the other end of the line, Michelle's grandmother rattled off every payment she made, and challenged the representative to highlight the missed payment - of course; there wasn't one[26]. This may seem like an innocuous mistake, but mistakes have proven costly to many borrowers. Sherry and Michelle's stories have far-reaching consequences that any of us realize. For many who've watched their relatives or friends get shortchanged by the financial systems, one lesson becomes apparent - loans are bad. Sherry vowed never to get loans, while

Stanley Fenelon[27] was taught by his parents to make sure that he was "independent," i.e., without any debt.

This misconception that "all debt is bad" has been a message I've had to live with my entire life, even though I chose not to heed it. My mother always made sure that our expenses just skirted the limits of her income, and when I started making money, she had a firm grip on my finances as well. Getting into debt was forbidden, and after I managed to pay off my ill-advised credit card balances, I was banned from any and all forms of borrowing - even from friends and family. I was to be "independent," as Fenelon was taught. Black Americans and other minority communities are less likely to apply for loans, mainly because of the discriminatory lending practices that have permeated the industry. The 2008 financial crisis blew wide open the world of subprime lending, revealing that minorities were more likely to be issued these loans compared to the white community.

However, despite the odds stacked against us, Black communities are rallying to fight the system, finding ways to pass on the right information. Contrary to what we grew up believing, not all debt is bad. However, the difference between good and bad debt is not as clear-cut as many people make it out to be. Because of the differences in our financial positions, needs, goals, and aspirations, one person's "bad" debt may be "good" debt for another person. But this is not meant to be discouraging. Rather, it is a wake-up call for us all to be more proactive when choosing to take on debt.

In essence, good debt is considered to be an investment, as it brings more income than it costs in payments. Mortgages, student loans, low-interest loans, and auto loans are considered to be good debt, mainly because of their intrinsic value and ability to generate more income or benefit for you. However, there are still many factors to consider before diving into taking out these loans:

- **Do you need it: This probably seems like an obvious yes to many of us, especially since we are already considering taking out the loan. However, it is never really the easy answer. Many people have ended up taking out mortgages for houses they believed they needed, only to have a hard time keeping up with the property rates, upkeep, and interest payment. It is easy to decide to get the house you love, but do you really need it? Can you be comfortable with a smaller, more manageable home?**

This also applies to auto loans and business loans. We get so caught up in getting the "best" that we end up choosing expensive cars and getting large loan amounts just because we qualify for them. You're better off living in a smaller house for a few years and upgrading when you need to, and this is the same case for a car.

- **What is the return on investment: The measure of good debt is what you get in return for it. Mortgages are considered to be good debt because of the value the home holds. Property prices are generally going up, so owning a home is a great way to start generating wealth. Additionally, renting out a home can help cover the mortgage payments, and owning rentals is an income generation venture in itself.**

Student debt is also considered a great investment, as we expect our value in the market to go up because of the qualifications we accrue. However, as the student debt crisis continues to balloon, it is worth mentioning that not all student debt is a wise investment decision. A CNBC poll found that 52% of millennials don't think their student loan was worth it. We have been conditioned to believe that a college degree will open doors for us, and the higher the qualifications we have, the greater our chances of getting lucrative careers. Kendra Brooks[28], a mother of four, believed the same when she decided to get an MBA from the University of Philadelphia. She happily took on more debt because she knew it would translate to a better salary. This was not the case. In a few years following her graduation, she had fallen behind on her payments, as her salary increase was barely enough to help her cover her children's needs and pay off the debt: "I had exhausted my savings, I lost my house, lost everything."

Not all degrees are the same, so you need to pay attention to the market rate for new graduates as you take on your student loan. For example, a fine art degree is unlikely to yield the same return on investment as a law or finance degree. According to Carrie Schwab-Pomerantz, a financial advisor, board chair, and president of the Charles Schwab Foundation, you should not take on more than what you expect to earn in your first year on the job[29].

- **Can you afford it: Just because a loan falls within your budget range doesn't mean you can afford it. For most people, making the downpayment always seems like the biggest hurdle, but forget that the ensuing payments will be recurrent, unlike the initial payment. The 2008 financial crisis was the culmination of the snowball effect of Adjustable-Rate Mortgages (ARMs). For many borrowers, the initial cost of taking the loan was too tempting to resist. They could put down as little down payment as they needed, and the interest rates were below market value. The loans were cheap and affordable - or so they seemed. When**

the interest rates inevitably went up, obviously above market rates, many borrowers were unable to keep up with their new payments.

Incurring any debt, even if it is good debt, requires vigilance on your part. Even good debt can become bad if we don't take the steps to ensure that they remain manageable. Make sure you pay attention to what you're borrowing, how much it is, and how the payments will translate in the long term. Can you sustain the loan with your current level of income, or are you banking on a future income projection that is not guaranteed? I am not telling you not to dream big. I'm only cautioning you against depending too much on a future income. You need to be a logical dreamer, not a head-in-the-clouds one.

Bad debts are the bane of our existence. They are the reason we stay up all night obsessing over how to get out of the hole we dug ourselves into. Bad debts have a way of staying in our lives for so long we sometimes just accept them as part of our financial destiny. Any loan is potentially a bad loan, as the credit card and student debt crises show. However, there are debts that are inherently bad, their very nature is meant to keep us paying exorbitant amounts in interest when we initially took out what seemed like an innocuous amount. Loans with high or variable interest rates, payday loans, loans taken out for discretionary purchases, credit card debt, and loans taken out to fund consumables, are all loans that we should strive to avoid. Paying off these loans is almost impossible, as late fees and penalties tend to snowball quite quickly.

When I got my first credit card, I was a naive 16-year-old making a few dollars per week. My mom had just attended a seminar about financial freedom, and she wanted me to start building up my credit score. She kept the card and would let me use it once in a while, mainly for groceries when we were running low. She'd then pay the balance as soon as she got paid, and we'd rely on my check for a little while. When I turned 18, I could get a card on my own, and I was ecstatic. I fell for the oldest trick in the book - the 0% banner that was flying above the booth in the mall. With pep in my step, I quickly signed up. "Every time you use this card, you get reward points," he said with a smile. I was sold. How I went from a single maxed-out card to three cards by 20 was a mystery to me. To avoid late fees and penalties, I used the revolving card method - use one card to pay off the balance of the other one. It didn't take long before I was in over my head. I couldn't tell my mother about it, so I did what I did best - got another card. The irony of my actions is not lost on me either.

The grip of bad debt is so tight that many people do not see a way out. As interests pile up and fees accrue, desperation finds a way into our hearts. Paychecks can barely cover the payments, and we still have to live. This has opened the market for a new predatory lending system that is disrupting the lives of many middle to low-income families. Payday loans are arguably one of the worst lending options to exist. For people who have poor credit scores and can't access traditional loans, payday loans seem like the saving grace they have been praying for. With attractive introductory rates, minimal qualification requirements, and quick disbursement, payday loans have helped so many people when they need money fast. However, with interest rates that snowball quickly, it is often difficult for payday borrowers to catch up to their payments. Most end up paying more in interest than the initial amount borrowed.

Debt, whether good or bad, keeps us tied to it for as long as we need to repay it. While good debt may lead to financial freedom, this cannot be said for bad debt. Millions of people are stressed out because of their financial obligations, and this curtails their ability to be free. Financial freedom is a long and arduous journey, and for some, it means sticking to a job they hate because it covers the necessary expenses. But how do we break from this mold? How do we scratch, fight, bite, and claw our way out of the hole we've dug ourselves into? How do we finally find ourselves staring at the hope on the horizon? Let's explore some of the ways we can eliminate bad debt for better peace of mind.

The Way Out is Through

For the Black community, debt has become just another chain dragging us behind, and the bias and discrimination we face in the workplace and financial institutions are keeping us from finding our footing. According to data from the 2007 Survey of Consumer Finance, single Black women in their working prime have a median net worth of $5[30] compared to $42,600 for single white women. Since we are more likely to come from low-income families, Black women have relied on student debt just to get the chance to rise above the fray. The average federal student loan, as of 2020, is $37,113, but as many Black women will confess, the amount they owe is much higher. Black women have the highest average student debt, but discrimination and bias at work see them reap less than their peers, earning just $27.76 an hour in 2020 when they hold a bachelor's degree, while white women made $32.02[31]. With advanced degrees, the pay stood at $37.75 an hour, $7 less than white men who only held a bachelor's degree. While we have been conditioned to believe that education is our way out of the trenches, once we graduate, we are faced with even greater issues as we work to pay off the loans that were supposed to set us free. The picture painted is much grimmer, as Black women are more likely to see their student loans grow, rather than shrink, after graduation. According to the Education Data Initiative, 48% of Black graduates owe about 13% more than they borrowed just four years after graduating, and 30% of Black college graduates default on their student loans just 12 years into their repayments.

With 3.5 million Black families having a negative net worth[31], it is in our best interest to find ways to beat the system that strives to keep us locked in the dungeon, swirling in the murky waters of debt. To find our way to the dry ground, we have to admit that things will be difficult before they get better. We have to learn how to make the painful yet proactive financial decisions that will help us sleep better at night. We have to let go of all the preconceived notions about who we are and what we can't do, and rise to the challenge. The first step of financial freedom? Getting out of debt. The simplest way to get out of debt is to make more than you spend, scrimping every extra coin and using it to clear the problematic balances that keep you up at night.

Here are a few ways to dig yourself out of the hole:

- **Focus on reducing expenses: It is hard to imagine how to achieve this when you are barely making do with what you currently have. This is why it will always be difficult for most people to get out of the**

cycle of debt. Cutting out expenses is an extreme sport, one that requires an obsessive level of focus on every single transaction, and constant trade-offs. Switching to generic brands, downsizing, getting a used car, choosing home-cooked meals instead of takeout, cheaper phone plans, and fewer subscriptions are just some of the ways to cut expenses.

By finding ways of reducing the cost of utilities and everyday expenses, you get to scrimp these extra dollars and redirect them to your debt payments.

- **Start with the bad debts: Because of the high fees and interest rates, it is best to tackle bad debt first, essentially cutting off the greatest and fastest leak in your financial portfolio. Review all your debts, and give them priority tags depending on which one has the highest penalty and fees. Once you have this figured out, highlight the minimum payment for each loan. The goal here is to try and stop the other loans from multiplying, while making sure that every effort is concentrated on eliminating each debt based on its overall interest rate.**

As you make regular payments, you get to build up a show of good faith with your lender, as you will need it when trying to negotiate a better repayment plan. No lender wants their customer to default, and by showing that you can be trusted to pay your dues, the representative may be able to help you secure a slightly better deal. However, this doesn't mean that the extra dollar is disposable income. Rather, it should be used to pay off the outstanding balance. By eliminating each debt, you get to pay off the other loans in bigger chunks. The goal is to make sure that the debts are cleared as soon as possible.

If possible, you may also choose to consolidate your bad loans by securing a low-interest personal loan and using the money to pay off the outstanding balances. This way, you only have one single chunk to pay off, at a lower APR. Of course, don't borrow more than you need.

- **Fix your credit: Poor credit scores not only have a negative impact on your finances, but also on your ability to secure good housing, better employment, and favorable deals. To fix your credit, you have to objectively analyze your credit report, finding the problematic areas that need fixing. If your debt to income ratio is greater than 50%, you need to focus your attention on debt reduction. Avoid applying for multiple lines of credit, and only borrow what you already have in your bank account so that you can pay it back without**

incurring fees and interest. Fixing and improving bad credit may be a long process, but you need to stick with it.

Develop the habit of borrowing less, making sure never to max out any credit card, paying your dues on time, and eliminating any additional lines of credit you may have.

•   Redirect your efforts to increase your income: An income increase is the fastest way to crawl out of the hole, but it has to be supplemented by all the other debt reduction methods. For most people, however, an increase in income rarely translates to financial freedom because of lifestyle creep. As you work your way to better pay, monitor the changes to your expenses. Curb any discretionary spending that doesn't involve clearing your debt or generation of more income.

We have the odds stacked against us, but as Black women, we are built to thrive. Financial freedom is achievable, but we have to give ourselves the chance to fight for it. We need to accrue as much financial knowledge as we can, and use it to beat the system that seeks to bite a chunk out of us at any turn. We need to wade through the murk, using our experiences as the spark that ignites our motivation to create a better, debt-free future.

Chapter 4 – Starting to Stack (0-$10K)

"Budgeting is not just for people who do not have enough money. It is for everyone who wants to ensure that their money is enough."

~ **Rosette Mugidde Wamambe**

Budgeting for Financial Freedom

Getting out of debt is not an easy process. We have to be intentional about our finances, attentive, and sometimes obsessive about our expenses. I have to admit that I only got out of debt because of the way my mother decided to go full attack mode. She ripped the bandaid off, and for the first few months, I was convinced that she was intentionally making me suffer. Her game plan was pretty simple - only buy what is necessary. Since I had used my own credit cards to create the mess by myself, I was solely responsible for the cleanup. We'd been planning on moving out of the tiny home, but she put a stop to it. "Until we have your balance on the green, we are staying put." That was it - no discussion, no negotiation. She didn't give me a chance to cry about it or promise to do better. Pen and paper on the kitchen table, she listed every single expense we had, including Justin's baby care needs. Next, she crossed out every bill that she paid for, leaving only the bills I was responsible for, and my debt. Then she folded up that piece of paper and threw it in her purse. I was terrified. And for good reason.

The next day, my mom unfolded the paper, and my worst nightmares came to life. The paper had notes all over it, apparently written by the church's accountant. It was the battle plan curated for my benefit. My entire salary from the club was to be dedicated to debt repayment, and I was to survive on the tips I made - which at the time weren't much. The first three weeks were hell. I was an average waitress, doing the bare minimum to make sure I wasn't getting fired. I'd looked down on the other colleagues who were pulling all the stops to get better tips, sure that I would never be in their position. I was content to coast through the work. In a single day, this changed. If I was to live properly, I needed to get the tips. My income from the beauty store was Justin's upkeep. I needed my own. It wasn't until I was in college that I realized what my mother had done was genius. She'd forced me to be comfortable with the bare minimum, to pay myself first, and to clear up any liabilities before incurring any further expenses. She'd created a very specific budgeting system that fit my needs, and forced me to become a better employee. To let go of the faulty identity beliefs I had, and to realize that my ego did not matter, when I needed to do better for myself.

I've met and read about many people who, like myself, approached restricted spending like a trip to the gallows. In many forums, I see people maintain that they cannot possibly stick to a budget. That it's too restrictive, that it limits one's experiences in life, or that it is impossible to maintain for a long time. To some level, I agree. Budgeting can be a painful activity, especially when you are forced to face your own shortcomings. It requires honest introspection and challenging your own self-imposed beliefs. How many times do you tell yourself that you don't have time to cook your own dinner or create a budget, but spend hours watching a show on TV? How many times have you told yourself that the generic item is low quality, and yet you've never tried it? "I can't use that," "It's too small," "I don't like the look of it," etc., are some of the conditioned beliefs we harbor that keep us in a loop of unnecessary spending.

While you can curate your budget to fit your lifestyle, this is a luxury that is only available to those who have the wherewithal. The ones who have crawled out of debt, have sufficient savings, and enough disposable income to let go of any future worries. For the rest of us, budgeting is a necessary tool. It is the stepping stone to intuitive spending, informed borrowing, and conscious saving. It is the life jacket that keeps us afloat as we make our way to shore. Budgeting has never been, and never will be a way of torturing ourselves. Our budgets are in fact our accountability tools, our safe haven.

Let's take a look at some of the more popular budgeting options, and you can decide which one best fits your needs:

• The Needs/Wants/Savings Budgeting System

I have always been fascinated by this budget system because of its simplicity. Also known as the 50/30/20 budgeting system, its premise is simple - split your expenses into three major categories; what you need, what you want, and your savings/investments. Half your income is dedicated to paying for your necessities - groceries, housing, utilities, gas, etc. 30% of your income is dedicated to your entertainment needs and the things you want, but don't necessarily need - streaming subscriptions, entertainment, dining out, vacations, etc. The last of your income is for your savings or investments.

The simplicity of this budgeting system makes it easy for beginners to implement, as it provides a general idea of how much you spend on various categories. However, this generalization is also this system's greatest pitfall. Because the allocations are so generalized, it is easy to spend money on unnecessary items as long as the limit is not exceeded. However, what happens when you begin earning more? For many of us, our expenses will increase within each category because of the increased income. Once this happens, it is easy to revert to our old ways. This system also fails to show us where our problematic expenses lie. Are you paying too much for some services? Are you allocating the most you can to pay off your debt?

This is not to discourage you from using this system, as it is a great starting point for those who are afraid of adopting restrictive budgets, or for those who need to start slow and build up to a budget that meets their needs.

• Zero-Based Budgeting System

This budgeting system is also great because of its simplicity, but it is a bit more detailed, and time consuming, compared to the 50/30/20 system. This system is founded on a simple concept: "No dollar goes unaccounted for." This is the system I currently rely on because of my ability to turn into a kid with $100 in a store. If I am left unchecked, I can easily rack up hundreds of dollars of purchases in a few minutes. My "I want this" list is never-ending, and I am always adding things to it that I believe will make my life easier even though I am currently comfortable without them. My need to always upgrade is something that frustrates my mother because of how easily I get bored with items, especially electronics and decor items. After I completed paying off my debts, my restrictive budgeting program was no longer needed, but I had to find a system that fit my needs. Zero-based budgeting was it for me, even though mine has been tweaked over the years to accommodate the changes in my life.

So, what is the zero-based budgeting system? It is a budgeting process that requires you to create a comprehensive list of your expenses, especially the monthly recurring expenses. Instead of grouping your expenses, this system relies on the accurate representation of where your money is going. How much do you pay for gas, utilities, rent, groceries, dining out, subscriptions, eating out, delivery services, debt payments, savings, investments, clothes, shoes, etc? You get the idea. The goal of this budgeting system is simple - your balance should be $0 once you've completed assigning your income to each budget item.

The zero-based budgeting system is great if you have a habit of making impulse purchases or making payments based on your perceived "needs" at the time. By having a clear idea of what your recurring expenses are, you can plan out the next month's expense chart in advance, and find room for items you may want without having to dip into your savings. If you're looking for help starting on your zero-based budgeting journey, apps like YNAB and EveryDollar will be a great start.

● Envelope Budgeting System

I absolutely adore this method, as it was the system that my mother tweaked and turned into the godsend that liberated my finances. The envelope system is a great fit for those who have an issue with overspending or managing their money. It can also be a great teaching tool for parents who want to show their kids how to be responsible and intuitive spenders. Much like the 50/30/20 system, the envelope budgeting system splits your income into broad categories, although you have the choice to create categories that are more specific. The traditional envelope budgeting system requires you to withdraw your income from your account, and use cash to make your payments and purchases. Once you have the cash, get multiple envelopes, with each bearing the name of the expense category. Put the amount of money in each envelope as needed, including the savings/investments/debt payments categories.

Once you've exhausted the money in a particular envelope, you have to wait for the next budget period to refill the envelope. You cannot move money from one envelope to another even if the envelope has money left over. If this happened because of your miscalculation, tweak your budget for the next period to reflect the new calculations. If you have debts, the money left over from any envelope is to be used to repay the debt.

However, I have to acknowledge that using cash in this day and age may be difficult, impossible, or too much of a hassle. If you'd like to remain cashless, find an app that has the envelope system. GoodBudget comes highly recommended, but it is a very hands-on app because it doesn't automatically sync with your bank accounts. With a free and paid version, you get the chance to try it out before committing to it.

● Incremental Budgeting System

The incremental budgeting system is definitely not for the faint of heart, as it requires absolute dedication to tracking your expenses, analyzing the changes, and applying these new changes to the next budgeting period. With incremental budgeting, your budget changes based on the previous period's/month's data. Although this budgeting system is simple because there are no complex calculations involved, it is time consuming and requires you to keep track of every transaction so that the next budget can reflect the changes in spending.

This system may shift to fit your needs, but if you have a problem with spending and/or poor money management, this budgeting system is definitely not for you. It will give you the perfect excuse to keep tweaking your budget to incorporate your spending habits, completely annihilating the purpose of budgeting.

Budgeting, like most things in life, does not have a "one size fits all" system. Your needs may in some ways resemble others' needs, but the details are wildly different. To find the budgeting system that will address your needs is a process that requires you to start by adopting the system that addresses your most fundamental goal - are you looking to be debt-free, save more, curb unnecessary expenses, or just track your expenses? By identifying your main goal, you can adopt one budgeting system in its traditional form. However, as your needs evolve, you can adopt a different one, or incorporate aspects of other systems to create a unique system to serve your needs.

When I adopted the zero-based system, I'd spend every penny that was dedicated to the category. I'd eat out just to make sure my entertainment fund was used up, and I'd buy items with any grocery money left over. I did this for a few months before I decided to incorporate the incremental budgeting system's fundamental aspect - changing the numbers based on the data available. However, I did put a spending ceiling on each category of expense. My goal has always been to spend as little as possible, and any money left over is transferred to my savings category at the end of each budgeting period. This allowed me to save, invest and become financially free and attaining freedom of time, which is far more important to me than having the latest heels or handbag.

There is no system that will fit all your needs, so you need to take it upon yourself to find your footing.

Recognizing Income Opportunities

Achieving financial freedom is a simple two-step process: minimize expenses and increase income. It's the execution of this process that's plagued with challenges because we are human. We are driven to find comfort, and our minds are susceptible to the suggestions of what is comfortable or acceptable. I have found myself making questionable decisions with my finances because of what I've seen on social media. I once bought an L-shaped couch because of a home makeover video I watched on YouTube. At the time, though, I believed that I was making the decision because the couch would be better suited to my apartment's layout. A few months later, I was watching a show where a carpenter was reupholstering an old 50s couch. When he completed the tufted design, I immediately began thinking I should get one of those because it looked so beautiful. That was a lightbulb moment for me. I paused the video, stood up, and began taking account of the things in the apartment. It didn't take long for me to realize that most of my purchases were not made because of necessity. I rationalized most of my purchases, repackaging someone else's decisions as my own. I had changed my dining table because I wanted a beautiful circular rug, so a round table was a better fit. The only consolation I had at the time was the fact that I'd sold my older pieces, and in the process, I'd learned the value of keeping my things in impeccable condition.

My grandmother was notorious for her reluctance to spend money, but it was her ability to sell things that bordered on traumatizing. She was a lifetime thrift shopper, and there was a reason cookware, plates, cutlery, and furniture in the home were mismatched. One Christmas, I think I was seven, my mother decided to surprise my grandmother with a new cookware set. She'd saved up, thinking that my grandmother would appreciate the gesture since all her pots and pans were dinged up, discolored, and featured an infinite amount of scratches. My grandmother received the gift with a look of pure confusion. She thanked my mother for her thoughtfulness, but she seemed distracted. After dinner, as my mother was leaving, she asked her how much the set had cost. When we came back to visit on New Years' Day, the set was nowhere to be found. She'd sold it to a church friend. My mother was livid, so she decided to complain to my aunts. Turns out my grandmother had sold every single gift she received, including the compression socks she'd gotten. When she passed away, we shared stories about how she would sell anything and everything, laughing as we reminisced. However, it quickly became apparent that she'd influenced all of us.

My cousins and I have been trading items since we were teens, and this habit has never died out. We take our clothes to thrift stores, we're regulars at the local pawn shops, and Facebook Marketplace has been a godsend to our family. I am now a "minimalist," but not because it's a lifestyle movement. I rigorously audit everything in my apartment every few months, and anything I don't use is immediately sold off. I am still amazed by the things I manage to sell.

Supplementing your income is not only about making thousands of dollars. It is about finding ways to ease your financial burden, one dollar at a time. The internet has given us tremendous opportunities to add a few dollars to our names, and it's time we make use of these opportunities. If you've sold everything you don't use in the home, it's time to focus on the value you can add to the world. What skills do you have? Are you good at writing, or crafts, or are you interested in more upcoming opportunities like dropshipping? I usually find myself watching craft TikToks, and I am always amazed at the creativity and ingenuity of small business owners. I have seen how cleaning has been turned into a budding business idea, how the same market has spawned niche options to diversify the competition, and how short videos have been turned into monetized YouTube tutorials.

I believe that there is always space for us and our ideas, and you shouldn't be discouraged until you start. When one of my college friends - let's call him Travis - joined a freelance transcription service, he was a 36-year-old line cook struggling to find some way of paying for the final year of school. His boss had promised to pay college tuition for him, but had to back out of the deal when he had health issues and needed the money to pay for his own medical expenses. Travis was absolutely wrecked by the news because he knew that he'd never get another chance to go back to school if he dropped out. He was used to listening to audiobooks at work, and believed he had a good ear for transcription jobs. In the first three months, he only had five jobs on the site, and despite his family asking him to find something else, he focused on honing his skills. On his days off, he spent hours transcribing audio as practice. Six months after he started, his work queue on Rev was insane. He quit his line cook job and focused on the better paying freelancing work. Several of my classmates, looking to cash in on the same service, quit just a few weeks into it because they were not getting any jobs, or the work was taking up too much of their time.

Currently, there are a host of sites that give us the opportunity to showcase our talents, including Upwork, Fiverr, Rev, Etsy, etc. If you have time to spare, working as a freelancer is a great way to increase your income, especially if you are willing to deliver top-notch work. While websites like Fiverr are slammed for shoddy work, I know of freelancers who have managed to use the website and earn a comfortable living making more than they would have in a corporate job. As with any other job, quality and consistency will be your greatest asset.

But before we dive into how you can turn these extra jobs into viable income streams, let's explore how you can make the most out of your current job.

Chapter 5 – Becoming Wealthy Through Your Career ($10K - $1MM)

"I am a woman who came from the cotton fields of the South. From there, I was promoted to the washtub. From there, I was promoted to the cook kitchen. And from there, I promoted myself into the business of manufacturing hair goods and preparations....I have built my own factory on my own ground."

~ Madam C.J. Walker

We live in a society that has become so obsessed with the concept of "side hustles" and passive income that we seem to forget the most important part - for there to be a "side," there has to be a "main." How do you approach your current career? What do you think of your job? How do you feel about the work you do? I have been involved in countless career-focused conversations, at work, in social settings, in school, and at home. I can count on one hand the conversations that were positive - where the person I was talking to was gushing about their work, excited about a project, and generally content to work towards their targets. One person was working in a fast-food joint, and I was absolutely flabbergasted by how excited he seemed at the prospect of becoming a manager. "Don't you want to do something else? The fast-food industry is hard work and has poor pay," I automatically responded. He stared at me for a few moments, and I could see that he was confused by what I said. "What do you mean?" he asked, and I went on the normal rant about the low pay, how he must be having a hard time paying bills, the long hours, and the "difficult" customers. He remained silent long enough that I started fidgeting, looking for an out from the conversation.

"I am a high school dropout, I have my parents to take care of, and my job gives me the chance to do so without having to take out loans. I worked construction, and all day I would pray for a job that wouldn't put me at risk of injury because I am needed at home. This job was a godsend for me, and I am not about to sh** on it because other people believe it's beneath them," he responded. I was just about to apologize when he added: "Don't apologize. I understand where you come from, and I can't fault you for thinking I'm like the rest of them. My coworkers are just like you. They are in the restaurant just until they get something better. I'm where I want to be, and I am needed here to make sure when the others come, they have me to show them the ropes." It had been a while since I was rendered speechless. I had nothing to say in response, so I just focused on asking him questions about his family and sharing stories about the types of customers we'd both had to deal with.

While I have never met him again, his story stuck with me. He'd accepted his place in the world and was content with the work he was doing. Most likely he's climbed the restaurant ladder and is earning well. When I came across Max Ehrman's *Desiderata*, I was awed by the line: "Enjoy your achievements as well as your plans. Keep interested in your own career, however humble; it is a real possession in the changing fortunes of time." Most of us don't really like our jobs, but we are stuck because of a host of reasons, usually pertaining to our financial needs. However, some of us are in jobs that can give us a way to amass the wealth we need to finance our true dreams. The most common way of achieving financial freedom through employment is by climbing up the proverbial corporate ladder, which usually comes with better pay, perks, and benefits. This upward mobility, while achievable, requires your dedication to the work, the company, and your team. Rising above your peers requires that you stand out from the crowd, proving why you deserve it. If you have dreams of rising up the ladder, there are ways you can fast track your journey to getting promoted:

• Create a Detailed, Foolproof Plan

"Where do you see yourself in five years?" is a question that triggers many of us, especially since there are so many changes we go through in a short period of time that it seems pointless to plan that far ahead. However, when it comes to our careers, it is advisable to have a general plan, a goal that we're heading for. If your goal is to achieve success in the traditional sense, i.e., climbing up the corporate ladder, you need a detailed, actionable plan that will push you up each rung. Is the career of your choice a good fit for your skills and interests? Is there room for growth within the career? How about the company of your choice? Does the company support faster upward mobility? Does the company offer a host of different opportunities? Does the company offer support to employees looking for better growth within the industry?

When Thasunda Brown Duckett started her career in the home equity industry, she made a choice many of us would berate her for - choosing the lowest paying offer she received from Fannie May. But Duckett had a clear plan, chose the offer that best aligned with her interests and skills, and worked her way up in the industry. Career success is marginally difficult if you're not invested in the industry you are in. Your genuine interest in the work usually shines through, as you'll be more amenable to learning what you need to learn to make yourself an even better candidate.

Once you've created a plan that answers the above pertinent question, set a timeline to achieve the goals you've set. Your plan should be realistic and adaptable, as there are always unforeseen circumstances that force us to shift our focus and direction. As your interests, circumstances, and achievements change, edit and revise your plan to reflect these changes.

• Take Ownership of Your Work

When we fake interest in anything, we tend to believe that no one can see past our well-constructed facade. Fortunately, or unfortunately, we are not really capable of faking it for the long term. "Fake it till you make it" is a popular saying, but it rarely works. It is only a matter of time before your true personality/intention shines through. The mask always cracks, sometimes with devastating consequences. This also applies to our careers. You may feign commitment to your work, but there's always a limit. This is why finding a career that aligns with your genuine interests is important. You are much more likely to weather the challenges and work to find solutions if you actually care about what you're doing.

Your commitment to your career is usually evident in the amount of effort you put in to produce quality results. When you consistently produce quality results - surpassing set goals, KPIs, quotas, e.t.c. - you increase your chances of snagging a promotion faster. Your commitment to your work should also span the entirety of the project, making sure that you understand and are well versed in every step of the process from the beginning to the end.

- **Embrace Feedback**

Performance evaluations can be a bi**h sometimes, and many of us dread having our work and personalities picked apart by our peers and bosses. Even though these evaluations do have their flaws, they serve a great purpose. We are naturally blind to our own faults and tend to believe that we are right. This is particularly true in the workplace, as we tend to nitpick others' decisions, questioning their thought process and way of doing things. However, learning how to embrace feedback is a great skill in the workplace, as it gives you a chance to reflect on your actions based on others' perspectives. They may see things you don't, and getting defensive right off the bat will deter them from helping you improve.

When you receive feedback, whether positive or negative, take the time to filter through it before reacting. The time you take to reflect on the comments will help you pinpoint your faults and find ways of working to improve on them. Additionally, the ability to receive feedback well is a great leadership skill, one that you will need when you get the leadership position you are vying for.

• **Become a Team player**

Interpersonal skills are important in any career. You will not be working in a vacuum, and your relationship with coworkers, clients, and other people you meet through your work matters. Treat everyone with respect, improve your communication skills (active listening and speaking), practice empathy, and be trustworthy. The easiest way to become a better communicator is to listen, understand, and fire questions back related to what somebody is saying. Often we get trapped in waiting for them to finish speaking so that we can get back to talking about ourselves or to add something we wanted to say. Instead of this, try to just listen and ask the other person as many questions as possible. This is a great hack to instantly improve your communication. These are just some of the skills that create a sense of cohesiveness within a team, allowing others to be ready to help you out because they know they can count on you. By becoming a great team player, you subsequently show the others in your team that you can be trusted to lead them. Hone your leadership skills while you are still in the lower rungs of the corporate ladder. You have no idea how soon it will come in handy.

• **Invest in Your Growth**

What are you doing to improve your marketability? Specializing in your field is usually a great way of fast-tracking your promotion or chances of getting better pay. However, in some industries, specializing might hurt your chances of marketability. Learning skills that make you flexible in your industry is also a great way of improving your marketability, especially if a leadership role requires oversight of different aspects of the industry.

Specialization and adaptability are two great ways to achieve self-growth, so don't stop finding ways to keep improving your existing skills and learning any emerging skills.

• **Take Initiative**

In some cases, it may be important to share your ambitions with your boss and/or people in the company who can help you find your footing. If you have a great boss who is invested in the employees' progress, sharing your own ambitions is a great way to find help from them. This may earn you the opportunity to get mentored, or exposed to the various opportunities present within the organization. I know of a friend who was shocked to find out that their company had a program where they'd foot the employee's school fees if they chose to pursue higher education. She'd been working in that company for six years and only found out about it after she overheard a junior associate talking about it on the phone.

Taking charge of your own fate is great, commendable even, especially if you follow through with gusto and the commitment you've shown in your work. This also works if you're looking for a pay raise. The answer is always no if you don't ask. So, gather your courage and fight for your compensation. Find examples of other similar jobs or employees (even at other companies) who are being paid more for a similar role, to back up your reasoning for a higher wage. If the answer is "no," you get the chance to ask what you need to do to get it in the future.

Word of caution: In your quest to rise up the ranks, be careful not to become a slave to your work. Working hard may be commendable, but hard workers are rarely recognized for their contribution, instead having more work piled on top of what they already have on their plate. The secret is to become a smart, efficient worker, purposefully utilizing every resource at your disposal to achieve the desired results without setting yourself up to be a doormat. Filter through the requests made by your colleagues to recognize who is using you and whose request is genuine. The purpose of efficient work is to give you time for other pursuits that will help you grow and nurture your skills and competence. Don't slack off, but don't overexert yourself either. Find a balance that helps you effectively fulfill your obligations while also allowing you to work on getting to the next level.

Choosing a career path is a process that cannot be undertaken lightly. While it would be marvelous for each person to follow their bliss and turn their passion and skill into a lucrative business or successful career, the reality is much more nuanced. For many people, their reality has been fundamentally different from the dreams and ambitions they harbored while they were young and ready to conquer the world. While I am now living the life of my dreams, I never imagined that it would turn out this way. I was average at best in Math, and my people skills were absolutely dismal. But as I discovered how good I was at managing the backend work in the beauty shop, I knew it was my best bet if I wanted to have even an ounce of the financial freedom I was craving. I have been part of my local church's young professionals meetups for years, and I have realized that as the attendees get younger and younger, I hear career options that I never thought possible, most of which even have the opportunity to work remotely from anywhere.

For many Black women, college is our Hail Mary, but the student loan debt becomes the shackle that pulls us back. However, this is not reason enough to quit before we start. The majority of Black women are in the healthcare industry, specifically in the home care niche. It's backbreaking work that has featured poor pay for decades, but the COVID-19 pandemic has created a massive shift in the way healthcare professionals are getting compensated. As the pandemic raged on, many healthcare providers came to the realization that they were not getting paid enough to risk their lives. As mass resignations began sweeping through hospitals and healthcare facilities, many employers were left with a massive employee shortage. Coupled with the fact that healthcare responders are now considered heroes, the public has also been calling for better pay. Amidst the chaos and instability, there are now new options for healthcare professionals - traveling nurses and home care professionals have greater demand, and so do other support staff in hospitals. If you're pursuing a career in the healthcare industry, keep your options open for these new opportunities that are unfolding as the needs of the public shift.

I am a massive consumer of financial videos, and I love watching Black women break down their finances, especially when they are brutally honest about their expenses. Many of the videos I've watched with incomes of over 80k a year have been in the **tech**

industry. There are so many different avenues within the tech industry, and I love watching as Black women not only pursue tech careers, but find their own success within a niche. Software engineers, programmers, data analysts, project managers, cloud engineers, and cybersecurity experts are just some of the most sought-after individuals. There are Reddit threads of tech experts recounting insane stories of how they are being recruited even though they already have jobs. Consider this if you are feeling a little cheeky - some people out there are working as many as 3 remote jobs at a time, in effect tripling their salary. It's fairly easy to just get along with a couple of hours per day in some jobs, especially when in a huge company of 10,000+ employees. Of course, do this at your own risk as if a company found out, you could get in trouble. The marketing world has also evolved, with social media calling for companies to adopt marketing campaigns that stand out among the thousands of ads that we see on a daily basis. Additionally, traditional marketing strategies are no longer as effective as we call for representation in the ads since consumers span different races, social statuses, ages, and communities. Black women are making an impact in the digital marketing world, and to better navigate the industry, companies are hiring more diverse marketing and social media administrators to create and curate their unique brand content.

81

Black women are also making their mark in the medicine, law, and engineering industries, but our number is still too low. The education quality disparity is keeping us away from industry, so we must do what we can to ensure that our daughters get the support they require when they show promise. Fortunately for future generations, industries are evolving, and we have more choices than ever before. Consider Lauren Simmons, the second Black woman to trade at the New York Stock Exchange, and the youngest person to do so. She worked for Rosenblatt Securities, only earning $12k a year. However, in a recent video by *CNBC's Millennial Money*[32], Simmons revealed that she's now earning approximately $650k a year. She left her full-time trading job after she was excluded by her peers and instead leveraged her media appearances, transforming herself into a financial personal brand. She is now an author, podcast host, and has had multiple TV appearances.

Leveraging Your Time and Experience

Simmons' new career path is not anything new, as many people have been able to leverage their experiences to create a new path for themselves. When the pandemic hit, many people found themselves working from home while others were unfortunate and lost their livelihoods. And as is common with major changes, the pandemic opened up a whole new world for many employees. With the commute time cut out of the day, many realized that there was so much more time left in the day to pursue other interests. For some, the distractions of the work environment were now removed, and they found that they could finish their daily tasks much earlier in the day. With the newfound time, many workers decided to leverage their time and make more money. For those whose companies didn't have tracking programs running on their computers, working a second job became a viable solution.

Working multiple remote jobs is a great way to stack up on your income, but before making this decision, make sure that you have carefully explored the pros and cons. On paper, getting a second remote job may seem to be the perfect solution, but there are multiple factors to consider, the most important being: *can you pull it off?* Even though remote work has less oversight, you still have to deliver quality, consistent work, and this takes time. Additionally, the workload may increase, requiring greater time commitment. Make sure that you check your current employment contract to ensure you're not in breach if you get a second job.

If getting another job is out of the question for whatever reason, this extra time is great for pursuing your own growth. Are there any other avenues for financial growth you could pursue if you got other certifications, training, or opportunities to gain experience?

The road to making your first million dollars may seem long, or even impossible, but Black women all over the country are finding ways to create wealth, often in creative and unique ways. You may choose to follow your career path, working your way up the corporate ladder, or you may follow your bliss and passion, creating a business that showcases your brand to its full potential. However, no matter the path you take, wealth generation means you have to be smart with your money. For Lauren Simmons, despite the major jump in income, her expenses have remained relatively low, approximately $5k per month. A big chunk of her money is invested in the stock market and other instruments, which is a great way to make it to the $1 million mark faster. Fortunately, we'll cover investing in detail in chapters seven and eight.

Before then, let's explore the ways you can create wealth through side hustles, online business, and other alternative income sources.

Chapter 6 – Wealth Through Your Side-Hustles & Online Business ($10K - $1MM)

"You don't make progress by standing on the sidelines, whimpering and complaining. You make progress by implementing ideas."

~ Shirley Chisholm

Having multiple jobs is not a new concept, as many of us have (or know people who have) held two or more jobs to keep up with our bills. Currently, terms like "side hustle" and "passive income" have become commonplace, with many people dreaming of the day they rake in enough money from their independent work to leave their boring and uninspiring corporate jobs. With the internet becoming more accessible, and social media providing a great platform to advertise skills and opportunities, launching a successful business has become a goal many aspire to reach. However, just like most things in life, getting your business to become a success requires consistent input and quality output. When your customers and/or clients find you reliable, they are more likely to refer their friends and become regular customers.

Many people think "passive" income requires minimum effort, but this is not always the case. We see the success of others and how they carry themselves and assume that it is just a matter of having enough capital to start the business. Behind the scenes is often a chaotic system full of madness that they may or may not have been able to tame. This is not meant to discourage you; rather, it is to remind you that what we see is sometimes a culmination of hard work and intense work to create an appealing aesthetic. So, if you are struggling to get a grip on your business when you start, don't fret. It is by stumbling that we get to learn how to walk. We are human.

Choosing your Hustle

Choosing a side hustle may be easy for some, but not for everyone. Like any business or venture, your side business should be viable, and your choice depends on what you're hoping to achieve. What is your end goal? For me, I wanted a more realistic look into how small businesses kept their books, to find out what my college books hadn't factored into the theory. I knew I would have to get employed by an accounting firm just to get the basics, but my weekends were mine to do as I pleased. The plan was to help out the businesses in my community while still having the freedom to pursue other avenues of interest. To achieve the professional growth I was aspiring for, I began approaching businesses whose owners were doing their own books. I charged below market price just to get the work, and as a way of convincing them to give me a chance.

For my mother, her side hustle was doing hair for her friends. She had been a hairdresser in her teens, but her work at the church had taken up most of her time, and she couldn't really hold down a second job. However, when we moved, she changed churches, and the new one was a bit more forgiving with its schedules and working hours. My mom hated braiding because of the time commitment, but she could do weaves pretty well. For three months, she spent her weekends at a friend's salon, helping out for just a small percentage of what the customer paid. When I asked why she was taking so little for the work, her answer was simple, "I can't be a threat, and I'm getting paid to learn what is trendy and the new sewing techniques." I quickly caught onto what she was doing. In six months, my mom was making wigs also, spending her weekends at her workstation in the living room. She'd found her niche market in the church, and congregants always had requests for wigs. Mom had to learn how to color the wigs, how to create cheaper and more expensive options, and create different packaging options for clients. She eventually had to completely stop doing weaves because she had no time to spare, and her return on investment was not as great.

My mother and I had a clear path to our side hustles because we were clear on our goals, and had the relevant skills required, although we both had to work on honing those skills before we finally achieved what we'd hoped for. Because of this, I always advocate for honest self-reflection before embarking on this journey. Here are some of the things you should consider as you figure out your path into self-employment:

- **What's your goal?**

"To make money…duh," may be your knee-jerk response, but take a moment to really think about what your intentions are with your business. The greatest joy is when the business becomes profitable enough to get us to quit our day job, but before it gets to this level, there has to be a reason why we are working on it. Starting a business, no matter what kind, is a process that is strife with challenges as we work to secure the necessary documentation, clients, resources, inventory, etc. Because of this, having a reason why you're doing it will give you the strength you need to push forth.

"When the going gets tough, only the tough get going" is a cliche quote that kept me working on my goal even on days when I questioned why I was putting myself through all the extra pressure, work, and sleepless nights. When choosing your hustle, reflect on your core reason, "the why." Are you doing this to grow your audience? To improve your skills? To grow your brand? To provide a much needed service? To innovate? To create? To improve your life?

Your reason why doesn't need to be complex. It just needs to have an impact in your own life. To be powerful enough that it can push you through the inevitable hard times.

• What do you need?

Every endeavor requires investment on our part, whether it's time, financial, or material resources. For me, I needed to find the addresses and contacts of the businesses I wanted to work with, which meant taking time in the evenings and weekends to visit the businesses and schedule a meeting with the owners. Additionally, I also had to source various materials to ensure that I had everything I needed to showcase my expertise. I got business cards, personalized notebooks, and proposals specifically made for the business I was visiting. Before the meeting, I had always spent time visiting the business and observing its front operations. I made assumptions based on my observations, which then informed my proposals. Many owners were happy to set me straight, and most were impressed that I'd actually taken the time to study their business. In some cases, I was given access to the store for an afternoon so that I could make the necessary adjustments to my documents. For every business I secured, it'd taken at least three weekends' worth of time to create what I believed was the winning proposal.

Some side hustles require more investment than others, and it is important that you look into this before diving into the business. For example, if you're looking into starting an Amazon FBA business, you have to factor in the storage & inventory costs, Amazon's policies, and how you can leverage Amazon's advertising platform to boost your business. When entering into the merchandise business, you have to consider the designs, the material you'll use, and the technology for transferring your designs onto the products.

Take your time researching your intended niche, but don't let the complexities deter you from going after what you want. We live in the information age, and you'll always find the necessary information to help you understand what you actually need, and how to avoid the common pitfalls that lead to failure. In this day and age, almost every side hustle can be found on YouTube, for free – and you can learn practically anything you like.

● Can you do it?

This is the most important question to ask yourself before you start off your business. If your business is resource-intensive, embarking on it if you are not too sure of your ability to commit will lead to inevitable failure. To gauge your ability to achieve what you've set out to do, create an actionable plan, taking into account every aspect of the business that requires your input, and those that can be automated. For example, if you're selling your crafts on Etsy, you need to take into account what you'll be doing to increase exposure for your products, as just posting them on the website may not be enough to set your wares apart from the others present on the site. Will you be making videos to showcase your process? Will you pay for ads on social media sites? Will you be boosting your products on the website? Will you be able to reply to customer queries in a timely manner? Will you be accepting customized requests?

Having a realistic picture of what your business will entail will help you find the best way to implement your ideas and goals without the risk of getting overwhelmed or disillusioned. Your wellbeing is paramount in getting your business to succeed, as you are better able to handle the nitty-gritty details with relative ease.

With the advent of the internet, starting a business is easier than it used to be, as we can always find information regarding what we may need, how to go about setting it up, the rules and regulations pertaining to the business, as well as the trends. If you're completely in the dark, tutorial videos are bountiful, as well as courses to help you get started. However, not all courses are on the up and up, so ensure that you perform your due diligence before forking out any money for a course. ***Keep in mind***: just because you see the course's ads on social media doesn't mean they're great. Always check the reviews on trusted websites.

Not all side hustles are created the same, but there are those that have gained popularity over the years because of the success people have been able to attain through them. Let's explore a few...shall we? Hopefully, if you haven't made a decision yet, this will help you determine which industry and option is a great fit for your skills and passion/interests.

• **Freelancing, Blog Writing/SEO Writing**

Freelancing has been a viable employment alternative for people for the longest time, as the freelancer is responsible for their workload, working hours, and pay rate. Recently, the availability of online marketplaces like Upwork, Fiverr, Rev, Guru, People per Hour, etc., has given freelancers the ability to provide their services on a global scale, and increased their earning capabilities. For me, Upwork and Fiverr became my saving grace when I had exhausted the number of local businesses I could work with. I still had free days because the work was not so intensive, so I signed up on these sites. I must admit that it took several false starts before I managed to get my first client, and I almost quit a number of times. With freelancing websites, you are competing against thousands of global freelancers, and it is your duty to set yourself apart from the rest, especially if you are bidding for the work. I watched countless videos made by freelancers on these sites to learn about writing the winning bid, creating an outstanding profile, and curating my portfolio to ensure clients could gauge my skills. It was much easier to get my second client after completing the first job, and with every positive rating I got, I was able to secure new and repeat clients, some of whom stuck with me for years.

Blog writing gained traction a few years back, and it's still a viable income stream today, mainly because of the affiliate links and advertising opportunities. There are so many niches to choose from when it comes to blogging, and the key is to provide a fresh and unique perspective, especially if your interests lie in popular fields like beauty, travel, fashion, lifestyle, etc. As blogging has become a competitive niche, it pays to find other ways to drive traffic to your website. It is not uncommon to find bloggers posting tutorial videos, hosting giveaways, or even behind-the-scenes videos. When your readers find ways of engaging with you, they are more likely to read your new pieces and recommend your blog to others. If you want to write blogs but have no interest in investing all your time in them, you can become a freelance blog writer, instead ghostwriting pieces for others. This allows you to build your portfolio while saving you the hassle of running your own page. Freelance bloggers, however, have to be versatile because the scope of their work is dictated by the client.

Online visibility for businesses and websites means greater organic traffic, which has a higher likelihood of translating into product purchases or increased ad revenue. SEO writing drives visibility, and in recent years, has transformed into a simple, yet powerful tool that needs highly skilled input. When I first heard about SEO writing about a decade ago, the focus was mainly on keyword density - the number of times the keyword appears. However, this led to an influx of websites ranking high on the results page despite the limited content and keyword stuffing they had. This called for a change in metrics, resulting in better ranking for quality websites that had great content that was well written, informative, and used the keywords in organic ways, incorporated into the content naturally. As businesses are competing for the prime position on search engine results pages, SEO writing/optimization has continued to be a sought-after service on freelancing pages.

Freelancing, Blog writing, and SEO writing - fortunately - can be done during your free hours depending on the client's requirements and deadlines. However, because of the lax oversight and supervision, embarking on this journey requires intense self-discipline and commitment to producing quality work each time. If you are prone to procrastination or have no interest in following directions provided by someone else, freelancing is really not for you. Success in these three industries requires consistency, dedication to excellence, and a commitment to learning about new and emerging trends to keep up with the competition.

● Shopify Dropshipping

In recent years, dropshipping has grown into a popular business model partly because of its relatively affordable capital costs, which has allowed many people to finally get the chance to run their own businesses. In essence, dropshipping is a business model where you act as a middleman between the supplier and the buyer. Once the customer has made an order on your store, you source the product from the supplier, who packages and ships the product directly to the client. Compared to traditional businesses, dropshipping is an attractive model because it spares you the costs related to inventory sourcing and storage, as well as packaging, handling, and shipping. This ease of entry is a double-edged sword, as dropshipping has evolved into a highly competitive market, and it takes dedication, understanding, and commitment to stand out.

Which products are you planning to sell? With dropshipping, there are countless options for you to offer in your store - a blessing and a curse. With a host of different choices, it becomes easy for you to stretch yourself thin in your excitement and in the process, drop the ball. Whenever I see an online store that offers everything under the sun, I rarely buy from that site unless the categories are well set up and organized. When you start out, you may be tempted to cast a wide net in an attempt to attract a wide array of customers, but this is a mistake you need to avoid. By choosing a specific niche for your store, you get to start small and work your way up as you better understand which products sell better and which products clients want you to stock. Additionally, the products you choose to stock will inform your choice of supplier(s). Suppliers can make or break your business, and there are as many reputable suppliers as there are shady ones. Carefully vet your chosen suppliers, and whenever possible, order samples of products you are selling to confirm their quality and the suppliers' shipping timelines. In dropshipping, suppliers are classically Chinese (to reduce your cost of goods), so bear in mind delivery to your customers can take a few weeks. The best place to start when looking for a supplier is Alibaba, or Aliexpress.

Your customers are the most important aspect of the business, and they can propel your store to new heights if you put in the time and energy to ensure that their issues are addressed quickly and queries are handled in a timely manner. Even the best supplier can make mistakes, but it is up to you to ensure that your client gets a satisfactory solution. Common complaints usually involve wrong, faulty, or damaged products sent to the client, missing products, excessively lengthy shipping times, or general dissatisfaction. While the mistakes may not have originated from your end, never blame the supplier. Own up to the problem and offer solutions quickly. However, if your suppliers' mistakes become frequent, it is time to find a new supplier.

To protect your store, put policies in place. Coming up with clear shipping and return policies, product descriptions, relevant disclaimers, service charges, etc., may seem like overkill when you're starting out and have few clients, but they are necessary. In addition to setting up the store, selecting products, and choosing suppliers, you need to market your products, create SEO based descriptions that give your products greater online visibility, keep up with the suppliers' inventory, and keep up with new trends, among other duties.

If you are looking for an income opportunity with minimum input, dropshipping is not for you. The industry's growth and intense competition has seen many people give up and call it a scam. Many online "gurus" tout dropshipping as an easy income source, distorting the expectation of many entrepreneurship hopefuls. Don't fall into the trap of expecting smooth sailing just because your store is set up. Your dedication, tenacity, and patience will ultimately pay off, but only if you put in the necessary work to ensure that your clients are getting the best possible service and value for their money.

● Etsy: Crafts and Merchandise

It's unlikely that anyone has not heard of Etsy, especially since it has become the go-to marketplace for people looking for antiques and unique items that match their taste, character, and quirks. For me, Etsy is a guilty pleasure, my go-to site when I am looking for unique gifts and decorative pieces. I have no artistic bone in my body, and it thrills me to discover uniquely beautiful items that I would never have come across in the stores within my neighborhood. My candle obsession drove me to one merchant's TikTok page, where I spent hours watching in fascination as she created absolute masterpieces with candle wax. While I am ashamed to admit this, I am still grateful for how Etsy took me down the rabbit hole into the beautiful world of crafts on TikTok and Pinterest. When one of my friends began making table mats, I was initially skeptical about how she would be able to scale such a niche product. The first year of her business was difficult, and I was barely able to keep myself from telling her to quit. However, as I watched her creations grow and evolve, I finally asked her why she hadn't quit.

Unlike many people who'd attended an Etsy workshop, Tamari (name changed for personal reasons) hadn't been looking to make a lot of money with her creations. For most of her life, she'd been unsettled, jumping from one venture to another, quitting whenever it got boring or difficult. She'd quit her blogging business three months into the venture, and quit her dropshipping business because she couldn't keep up with the logistics of dealing with multiple suppliers. She'd begun customizing phone cases and selling them on eBay and Amazon, but that got old fast. By the time she heard about Etsy, she'd been bored silly at her job, and was looking for somewhere to dispose of all the place mats she'd been making and experimenting with in her free time. The workshop, for her, was an opportunity to learn about the work that went into creating a store that stood out. She just wanted to make her free time more productive.

As she puts it, setting up her account was the easiest part of the project. What comes next is what will make or break you. Take time to optimize your profile. With a clear image of yourself or your logo as the business owner and a well-crafted bio, you get to introduce your customers to your brand and the reason why you started the business. With your social media profiles also linked to your page, curious clients get the opportunity to find out more about you and your business. Once she had her profile up, Tamari had something new to focus on - product photography. Clear shots of your product from multiple angles, coupled with a detailed and accurate product description, gives the client a realistic representation of what to expect. As is the case with online stores, your product description requires optimization to increase your chances of visibility.

Because Tamari was working a minimum wage job, she was responsible for every step of the process. Learning SEO writing, product photography, the best ways to package her products, shipping, and customer service, was not easy. And this was before she even realized that she needed to promote her products on various social media platforms. If you are interested in running an Etsy store, it is paramount that you understand the work that goes into running a successful store. Be prepared to have your time taken up by administrative duties, and use the first few months as a learning opportunity. What will work for one store may not be great for your store, and because of this, you have to be open to feedback, taking the time to understand your niche better, what works and what doesn't. My advice - do not rush the process. Etsy is a wonderful marketplace, and once you find your groove, you'll be wondering why you found it so challenging in the first place. However, your tenacity, adaptability, and grit will determine your chances of success.

• Amazon FBA Business, Amazon KDP, Merch by Amazon

Amazon has given many small businesses the platform to reach millions of customers all over the world, and with Amazon FBA, Amazon KDP, and Merch by Amazon, you have the option to choose which service best fits your needs. For many merchants, Amazon FBA is a godsend because of its relatively easy process. As the merchant, your work is to make sure your products are well represented on the website, complete with the relevant pictures and optimized descriptions. With Amazon handling inventory storage, order fulfillment, packaging and shipping, your focus remains on what is most important - making sure your fees and duties are paid on time, and your marketing efforts are well curated. With Amazon KDP, independent authors get the opportunity to compete with other writers globally, all while avoiding the hassle of dealing with traditional publishing houses. Amazon KDP has been great for my reading habit, as I have had the opportunity to discover new authors with fresh insights and takes in both the fiction and non-fiction genres. For many coaches, Amazon KDP has opened up a world of new clients, and the same can be said for various small business owners. And now, with Merch by Amazon, artists and creatives get the chance to have their designs printed on t-shirts & hoodies by Amazon, earning them royalties for every design purchased. Again, there are endless numbers of tutorials for both KDP and Merch on Youtube, from a wide variety of content creators.

Finding your way onto the Amazon platform is quite easy because of the countless people who've documented their journey through each Amazon niche. Before setting up your business and committing to inventory, take the time to get the information you need about the common mistakes and pitfalls that tend to trap newbies. Pay close attention to Amazon's policies, as these can change at any time, and violating the company's policies may result you losing your royalties that you were about to be paid.

● **Online Tutoring**

The level of competition among students in the world has become intense, and with the convenience that the internet offers, students get the chance to hire tutors from all over the world. In many Asian countries, for example, students strive to learn English because it gives them an edge over their peers. This has led to a boom in the English tutoring industry, with parents clamoring to find their children dedicated tutors to help them learn a new language. Other students need help understanding class material on various subjects, with graduate students also seeking help from experts who've been through the same process.

If you are able to, find a tutoring platform that caters to the services you're looking to offer. Many sites give you the chance to choose your lesson times, but if you're dealing with international students, make sure you're available at the required time. For many tutors working with Asian students, waking up at 3 a.m. is standard practice. If you have any reservations about your ability to provide the required service, don't embark on this journey. Many students tend to trust their tutors, and your mistakes could prove costly to their chances of success.

These suggestions are by no means exhaustive, and we've barely scratched the surface of the ones mentioned. Side hustles abound, and it's absolutely thrilling to watch as more and more Black women find niches that give them the chance to build their wealth. Take, for example, Breonna Johnson, [33]. Trained as a teacher, Johnson was working in a kindergarten, overworked and underpaid. When the pandemic hit, she found herself at a loss what to do, so she joined a nanny agency to find work as a part-timer as she waited for schools to reopen. However, she managed to see various opportunities within the industry, and decided to train as a new-born care specialist. With her education background and the additional certification, Johnson was able to leverage both for two nanny jobs in New York and Atlanta. With $175k a year and various benefits, Johnson has joined the FIRE (Financial Independence, Retire Early) movement. 25-year-old Wilglory Tanjong[34], a full-time Wharton School of Business MBA student, turned her handbag design side hustle into a luxury brand. Tanjong has made over $725,000 from this side business.

There is no single side hustle that fits everyone. It is up to you to discover what is right for you. For most people, however, it becomes much easier to turn your passion into your hustle, as you're already in love with the craft. You can also leverage your skill, turning it into an income-generating endeavor. I cannot tell you which side hustle to embark on, but I can assure you that you will never know which one will work for you if you don't try.

Chapter 7 – Understanding Company Structures & How to Sell your Online Business [$10K to $1MM+]

"Five to ten years ago, Black women wanted a seat at the table, and now Black women are building that table."

~ Nicki Tucker

The challenges Black women face in the workplace - discrimination, low pay, stagnating careers, bias, disrespect, propensity for getting furloughed, laid off, or taking pay cuts, etc. - have pushed many to try their luck as business owners. In 2021, LeanInc.org carried out a survey with 12,000 participants[35], in which 37% of Black women stated that if they lost their main source of income, they'd only be able to afford to pay for basic necessities for one month. For white men, only 21% had the same response. 39% of Black women had difficulties paying their bills in the 2020-2021 period, with 24% stating that the pandemic had devastating effects on their finances. Additionally,

Black women were twice as likely to say that they had been furloughed, had their hours cut, and took pay cuts during the pandemic. These reasons offer some explanation of why Black women are more entrepreneurial. While women of color only make up 39% of the female population in the country, they own 80% of women-owned businesses, with 42% of new women-owned businesses belonging to Black women[36].

However, even as we forge our own path in the entrepreneurial space, Black women still face major challenges pertaining to funding, scaling, or even getting their businesses to stick. Only 3% of Black-women owned businesses stick, compared to 7% of white-women owned businesses[37]. When starting their businesses, many Black women are already encumbered with student loan debt and other debts, have fewer resources, and lower collateral. Combined with the difficulties of obtaining financing and unaffordable advertising and marketing costs, the road to entrepreneurial success is not easy. But it is worthwhile. Finding the power in yourself to fight for your business, your livelihood essentially, is a feeling unlike any other. To date, I look back at the hard times and feel happy that I took the chance to head out on my own. I had to stay employed for five years to build up my nest, but the challenges of my workplace and side hustles were easier to bear because of the journey I knew I was about to embark on. My dream was to turn my freelancing business into a more streamlined incorporated business, but with the time constraints and limited budget, it made more sense to start small and scale as I grew my client base and diversified my services.

In this chapter, we'll explore the various types of businesses, from sole proprietorship to S-corp, to better understand the options available when you are ready to turn your side business into a real one.

Sole Proprietorship

This is the most common type of business for small business owners, primarily because of how easy it is to set up. As a sole business owner, the business may bear your name, and since it is not incorporated, all you have to do is comply with the state or city's permit/license requirements. If your business deals with taxable products, you need to register with your state; and if you have employees, ensure that you apply for the Employer Identification Number (EIN) with the IRS.

The sole proprietorship's biggest flaw is its inextricable link to the owner. When the business is doing great, you get to partake in the profits, only paying personal income tax from the profits earned. However, since there is no separation between you and your business, you have unlimited liability. The business' liabilities are your own, and your personal property can be used to pay off your creditors. This means that your home, car, and belongings are fair game when creditors come to collect what you owe them.

If you are just starting out, the sole proprietorship business model is a great way to start your journey, and you can always incorporate the business when the time is right.

General Partnership

Like a sole proprietorship, a general partnership business is also easy to set up and requires no incorporation. Setting up a general partnership requires an agreement between you and your partner(s) regarding the distribution of profits and losses, since all partners share unlimited liability. A general partnership is also common because of this ease of setting up, and it is just as easy to dissolve should you want to part ways.

Typically, all the partners in a general partnership are involved in the day-to-day operation of the business, and they all share responsibility for the decisions made by a partner - even if the other partner(s) were not aware of them. Taxes are paid on the income earned by the partners from the business, just like the sole proprietorship. Similarly, because the partners in a general partnership have unlimited liability, they remain unprotected from any lawsuits filed against the business, and their personal assets can be seized and used to cover any of the business' liabilities and unmet debt obligations.

A general partnership is a great starting point as you can choose to incorporate the business at any time in the future.

Limited Liability Company (LLC)

Governed by state regulations, which vary from state to state, a limited liability company is recognized as a separate legal entity from its owner. Because of this, the private assets of the owner or owners, known as members, cannot be seized to cover the liabilities of the company. Ownership of LLCs is open to anyone, including single owners, multiple owners, corporations, or even other LLCs.

To register your business as an LLC, first research your state's requirements and federal tax organizations. While there are variations in the requirements depending on the state, some commonalities do exist. Articles of organizations establishing the rights, duties, liabilities, powers, and other obligations of each member are filed with the state. There may be other information required, like the names and addresses of the members, the name of the company's registered agent, and the statement of purpose. Additional paperwork needs to be filed at the federal level for your business to obtain the Employer Identification Number (EIN). Relevant fees apply at both the state and federal level.

Just like the sole proprietorship and general partnership, LLCs also enjoy pass-through taxation, which is why this business model is widely popular for incorporated companies. With pass-through taxation, the business itself is not liable to pay taxes. Instead, the members file personal taxes based on the profits they have gotten from the business. There is only one single point of taxation for an LLC - at the member's level. Additionally, as a member, you can use the losses you've incurred in the business to offset your other income, but only up to the amount you invested into the business.

One fundamental flaw with the LLC pertains to its continuity following the passing or exit of a member. If there are no agreements in place created by the members, if a member passes or leaves, then the LLC has to cease operations. The remaining members, or descendants, are required to dissolve the LLC. If they want to continue operations, they have to form a new LLC. To prevent this, members can create a business continuation agreement, which can then be used to ensure a smooth transfer of interests following the death or exit of a member.

Because of its limited liability structure, the LLC may be a great choice for you. However, there are limitations to the "limited liability." If you make any **personal guarantees**, for example, when taking out a business loan or when creating payment agreements with suppliers, this trumps the legal protection provided by the state. For example, if you use your house as collateral for the business loan, then the bank can seize the house since this was stipulated in the agreement. Additionally, criminal activity and gross negligence also void the liability protection.

Limited Liability Partnership (LLP)

Why an LLP and not an LLC? While limited liability companies do allow for multiple owners (these can be the partners), there are some professions that require a more formal structure to the partnership. LLPs are usually common with lawyers, doctors, accountants, engineers, architects, and other professions that rely on reputation. General partnerships usually work in some professions, but the unlimited liability fails to protect the partners from each others' legal liability. For example, if one partner makes a decision that leads to a lawsuit, the other partners are equally culpable even if they had to hand in the matter. The limited liability, in this case, serves to protect the partners' personal assets because their business is a separate legal entity. If one member is found guilty of a crime or gross negligence, the other members are not implicated even if the business assets are seized to pay for damages.

However, this legal protection is just one advantage of an LLP. By pooling resources together, the partners share office space, administrative employees, equipment, etc., giving them the chance to reap higher profits than if they'd worked individually. This is especially the case in partnerships where all the partners bring in clients and are active in the day-to-day operations of the business. Additionally, the pooled resources allow the partners to hire enough employees to handle tedious tasks, giving them the chance to focus on getting new clients. With a partnership, scaling the business becomes marginally easier since the partners' time is reserved for more important tasks.

To set up a limited liability partnership, you need to file the necessary paperwork as stipulated by state and federal guidelines. Also, depending on the state, there might be variations regarding the extent of the limited liability the members have, so make sure you consult a lawyer about this. Because of its customized nature compared to an LLC, the LLP requires a written partnership agreement, and the business may be subjected to annual reporting requirements, which are stipulated by state regulations.

Point to note: not all partnerships have active partners participating in the day-to-day operations. Some partnerships may have a single member who wields all the power, with the others being silent partners who only have a financial stake in the business.

112

Corporation (C Corp)

A corporation is commonly referred to as a "legal person" because of the legal rights and responsibilities that they wield. A corporation is legally allowed to enter into contracts, take out loans or loan out money, to sue and be sued, to own assets, hire employees, and pay taxes, among other possibilities. Just like an LLC, a corporation may have a single or multiple owners. However, its incorporation is more complex and costly, requiring articles of incorporation to be filed by the state, in the case of a private or "closed" corporation. Public corporations are governed by federal laws, usually the Securities and Exchange Commission. The corporation also has to obtain the Employer Identification Number from the Internal Revenue Service. Company stocks are then issued to the shareholders, who may or may not have the power to vote. Typically, one shareholder is generally accorded one vote.

For corporations, oversight is usually done by a board of directors, who are chosen or voted in by the shareholders. The board of directors is then responsible for hiring and overseeing the senior management, who are responsible for the corporation's day-to-day operations. The corporation's most distinct feature is its taxation. Unlike LLCs and sole proprietorships, corporations are subject to corporate taxes - a tax on the profits before dividends are issued to investors. The corporate tax rate varies depending on the country, with some countries getting designated as "tax havens" because of their low corporate taxes. The corporation's two points of taxation - corporate tax and individual taxes paid on the income shareholders receive from the corporation - have been the subject of extensive debate, with many criticizing this double taxation. However, for some, the advantages provided by the corporation's legal standing far outweigh the tax issue.

Most corporations pay taxes that are lower than the statutory rates because of a number of factors, including government subsidies, deductions, and tax loopholes. For corporations, deductions range from operational costs like advertising, marketing, and business travel to medical insurance for family members and other fringe benefits. The deductions are usually applied at the discretion of the company's accounting teams. Because corporations are taxed under subchapter C of the Internal Revenue Code, corporations are usually referred to as C-corporations (**C Corp**). However, some corporations, if deemed eligible by the IRS, are classified as S-corporations.

- ### S Corporation (S Corp)

Upon meeting certain criteria as stipulated by the IRS, a corporation may be classified as an S-corp. Unlike the C-corp, the S-corp is not subject to double taxation. The S-corp qualifies for pass-through taxation, and its income, credits, losses, and deductions are passed to its shareholders without being subjected to federal corporate taxes. The shareholders then report these on their individual tax returns. This is the greatest benefit of an S-corp compared to a C-corp. However, to qualify as an S-corp, the corporation has to meet certain criteria, including:

- The corporation has to be incorporated within the United States (domestic incorporation)

- The corporation only issues one type of stock

- The corporation has no more than 100 shareholders

- The corporation's shareholders meet the set eligibility requirements - i.e., corporations, partnerships, LLCs, and non-resident aliens do not qualify as eligible shareholders

For shareholders, their self-employment tax liability may be lower because the income received from the business can be characterized as salary or dividends. However, compared to C-corps, S-corps are under much closer scrutiny from the IRS because the business may characterize salaries as corporate distributions to avoid paying payroll taxes. Therefore, the IRS usually checks whether the corporation is paying reasonable salaries before it makes its dividend distributions. Because of its shareholder restrictions, S corporations have scalability issues, especially if the business is growing fast. To obtain necessary funding and growth, an S-corp may need to change to a C-corp.

Choosing which business model to apply to your business depends on your current operations, as well as your future plans. I started my business as a sole proprietor, but I now have an LLC. There is no one "right" business model, but you need to be careful when making your decision. You can start as a sole proprietor and later incorporate your business, or you may choose to stick to your current model.

Quitting Your Job

For most of us who start side hustles, there comes a time when we start thinking about quitting our day jobs to focus on our own ventures. For me, this moment came after my weekends and evenings became insufficient to handle the new business I was getting - both referrals and through the online freelancing platform. When I started turning down more jobs than the ones I was working on, I realized something had shifted in my business. I needed to devote my time to growing the business, as more refusals would put a damper on the business growth. Granted, quitting my job at the time seemed like a stupid idea. Even with the new business, the income I would be generating would be less than my salary by about $300. My savings could only support me for about two months because of the lifestyle I was leading at the time. I still lived in a two-bedroom apartment even though my mother had moved out, my car was taking up a chunk of my salary to maintain and fuel since my job was about an hour's commute on a good day, I was ordering takeout on a daily basis because I had no time to cook, and sometimes I had to resort to hiring someone to clean my home and do chores around the house. For the most part, I was spending almost every single cent I made from both my job and side hustle to support my lifestyle. So I took the time to consider how my life would change if I decided to quit my job.

I loved my car and I was not willing to let it go, so I shelved any ideas pertaining to selling or trading the car for something better. My final plan included moving to a smaller home and getting shelves for my documents instead of using an entire second bedroom as an office, adopting meal prepping, and doing my own chores. Even with a reduction in income, I would be able to support myself because of the reduced expenses. The decision had been made - I was quitting. It took three months for me to finally quit my job, but I hit the ground running. I'd already moved - a whopping an hour and a half's commute away - to a residential area, but the rent was cheaper. My commute was minimal, so my car expenses were reduced.

My decision to quit was pretty straightforward. However, this is not the case for many people. So, when should you quit? The answer to this question depends on your unique situation, but there are a couple of factors you have to consider:

- **Are you making a "healthy" income?**

If your business is making at least twice your salary, then it's safe to quit. However, there are other considerations you can make even if your business is not at this level. First, define what a "healthy income" means to you. For some people, their income is already high, so getting the business to make twice that amount may take time. In this case, outline how much you actually need to live comfortably. Is your lifestyle optimized, or are there expenses that can be cut? With your business's current income, can you live comfortably without some of the luxuries you enjoy? The answers to this question require proper and honest financial planning.

If it will take too long for your business to make twice your salary amount, but you can live comfortably on what your business is bringing in, this constitutes a "healthy income." You can use this to make the decision to quit.

- **Do you have a savings cushion?**

Even with a healthy income, you have to have a

contingency plan in mind. Having a savings cushion will keep you going even when you face unexpected issues. The safe bet is to have at least enough to keep you going for at least six to twelve months.

- ## Are you ready and willing?

Your side hustle has proven to be a viable idea, and your plans show that it has sustainability power. However, taking the jump into the unknown is usually a scary premise. If you are not ready to leave your job, don't rush to leave it. However, your decision to stay has its consequences. The limited time dedicated to your business, opportunity costs, and scalability limitations are all trade-offs to remain in your comfort zone.

You may feel that you're not ready, and frankly, you'll never be. However, your willpower and resolve will push you to take the plunge.

Selling your Business

So, maybe by now you've spent a few years building up your online (or other) business - and maybe you're again finding yourself desiring something new. I feel it's important here to tell you in this section just how powerful selling your business can be. Because remember, **you can sell your business, but you can't sell your job income!**

There are multiple reasons why you may want to exit your business, including boredom, better prospects, retirement, or you are just ready to move on. No matter the reason, selling your business has to be a well-thought-out and planned process. Here are some considerations to make if you are looking to sell your business:

• How attractive is the business?

First and foremost, is your business profitable? Selling a business that's doing well is much easier than selling a business that's failing. Businesses with increasing Y/Y (year on year) profits, consistent income, and a strong returning customer base are attractive to potential buyers, so it's best to work on these before putting the business for sale. By increasing the value of your business, you get the chance to get the most out of the sale. Do you have assets included in the sale, maybe email lists, websites or domains that add further value? Do you have an SOP that details how your business works so that the new buyer can easily take over knowing what needs to be done? Do you have a plan to detail what improvements could be made to the business to further interest prospective buyers?

• When to sell

The timing of your sale is also important. Taking the time to prepare for the sale requires your commitment and input into making sure the business is at its peak shape. Is your equipment in working order? Are there any repairs to be made? Do you have the necessary documentation? Will you be sourcing help from brokers? Do you have the funds to hire a lawyer?

Once you've made the decision to sell your business, plan out every aspect of the selling process to establish a timeline for when everything will be in place. If you're planning on handling the sale yourself, you need to ensure that you have everything ready. If you'll be using a broker (for example empireflippers.com), set up a schedule that will allow for regular updates, follow ups, and proper compensation.

- **Business Valuation**

What is your business worth? The easiest way to determine the worth of your business is by using the profit multiplier method. This involves taking the net profits earned over a period of time, usually about a year, and multiplying it by a given factor. These multiples may vary depending on the industry your business is in, so ensure that you check the industry multiplier. The following image from [https://www.robotmascot.co.uk/ebitda-multiples-by-industry/] shows you some examples of *annual* multiples.

Use the table below to five the EBITDA Exit
Multiple for your sector

Industry	EBITDA Multiple
Advanced Medical Equipment & Technology	24.81
Advertising & Marketing	11.10
Aerospace & Defense	14.69
Agricultural Chemicals	11.48
Airlines	8.16
Airport Operators & Services	8.16
Aluminum	7.57
Apparel & Accessories	12.58
Apparel & Accessories Retailers	10.30
Appliances, Tools & Housewares	10.36
Auto & Truck Manufacturers	9.81
Auto Vehicles, Parts & Service Retailers	12.09
Auto, Truck & Motorcycle Parts	7.08
Banks*	20.56
Biotechnology & Medical Research	16.03
Brewers	15.54
Broadcasting**	8.76
Other Broadcasting	8.46
Cable Service Providers	9.66
Radio Broadcasting	8.46
Television Broadcasting	8.46
Business Support Services**	10.03
Call Center Services	9.73
Cleaning Services	9.73
Commercial Educational Services	15.17
Corporate Accounting Services	9.73
Data Processing Services	9.73
Exhibition & Conference Services	9.73
Health, Safety & Fire Protection Equipment	9.29
Industrial Design Services	9.73
Industrial Equipment Rental	9.73

From my experience, for an online business, you can currently expect to fetch around 35-50x the monthly profit figure. And in addition, the larger the business (i.e., if it's over 1M valuation), the higher your multiplier will be. While a 50x in the chart above months only represents 4.1 years if using the annual valuation method, so it may seem low; consider that you would still be receiving four years worth of income in one day - which is not insignificant. And like we said, you can sell your business but not your job salary! EBITDA simply means earnings before interest, taxes, depreciation and amortization, and earnings is just another word for profit.

However, this simple method may not factor in other variables that may enhance or reduce the value of the business. For example, if the business has non-transferable expenses, like a loan, deducting this expense increases the profit margin. Conversely, if the business success is reliant on your specific skill set or if it takes up too much time and cannot run with minimal supervision, this reduces its value.

For a better and more realistic valuation, it will be best to hire a business appraiser or broker. Their expertise gives them the chance to offer valuable advice regarding increasing your business valuation.

• **Documentation**

Proper documentation will help ease the selling process, and you'll save valuable time if everything you need is easily accessible. Financial statements, tax returns, a list of the assets/equipment/inventory included in the sale, and a contact list for customers and suppliers are just some of the documents that a potential buyer may need before making the decision to buy the business. It's also helpful to include a SOP (standard operating procedure) detailing exactly how the business runs, like a manual that somebody brand new could easily understand. However, because of the sensitivity of some of these details, it is best to also have a non-disclosure agreement (NDA) drawn up and signed by the potential buyer before providing the documents. Additionally, you may have a general information packet with information regarding how the business operates and any improvements that may need to be undertaken before the sale. This information packet should provide a general idea of what the potential supplier should expect regarding the sale and operation of the business without giving away too many details.

- **Finding a buyer**

Do you plan on using a broker or selling the business yourself? How urgent is the sale? Getting a buyer may be a long and arduous process, and you need to be prepared to wade through the offers received to find the best buyer. If you're planning on personally overseeing the sale, you need to factor in the time invested, and the trade-off incurred when the sale takes you away from the business. Paying broker commission may seem like a waste of funds, but they are the best bet if you're looking for a fast sale, or if your business cannot thrive without constant supervision. The choice is up to you.

Alternatively, you may list your business on online marketplaces, including empireflippers.com and quietlight.com. Broker fees at empireflippers for example, range between 15% and below, depending on the value of your business.

Generating additional income through side hustles and personal business is just one aspect of achieving financial freedom. What you do with this income is the second part of the equation. Creating wealth requires informed and well-thought-out investment plans. Saving is a good way of keeping your money, but why settle for good when you can aim for great? Let's explore the investment options available for you.

Chapter 8 - Investing Basics (Why Invest, ETF's & Market Cycles)

"Dear Black Women... Save, Invest, and Spend Less. Save because you just never know what will come up... Invest so that you'll have something of value to show for it. Investing also helps in building WEALTH."

~ Stephanie Lahart

For my family, saving has always been the ultimate goal, having a bank balance that we can stare at and go, "Wow, those are so many zeroes." For most of my 20s, all I wanted was to have thousands of dollars stashed somewhere, just like my grandmother. Well... not exactly like her, although I do remember my family's excitement as my mother and her siblings sat on my grandmother's dining table to split the couple thousand dollars they'd discovered stashed all over her house. I just wanted to have the money so that I wouldn't worry whenever I had to make necessary payments. I was tired of having to sacrifice one thing for another. Now, I feel lucky that I got to see that there was more to creating wealth than just having money in the bank. Investment always seemed like an activity reserved for the rich-rich, those getting courted by hedge funds and major investment funds, and the suburb-dwelling, McMansion-ing middle-class professionals.

Even as we covered an introductory class on investing, I was barely paying attention, choosing to retain just enough to pass the exam. I was convinced investing was expensive, and I didn't have that kind of money to spare, and it would be a long time before I did. And even if I did, why would I put my money where I could lose it? I am chronically risk-averse, and it took three colleagues to convince me to *at least* consider it. "Just take time to invest a little money that you would have spent on going out or entertainment," one colleague said. "Challenge yourself to do that, at the least." So, for six months, I pushed myself to spend less than was stipulated in my budget so that I could try. I wish this were a happy success story, where I hit it big on the first try. Unfortunately, I was lured in by the cheap price of penny stocks being promoted on a rogue online investment forum I'd joined, and without doing my due diligence, I put most of my money in it. To my horror, it turned out to be a rug pull. My colleagues couldn't hide their amusement even as I sat there seething. The irony of my situation did not escape me, but I'd learned my lesson. Fortunately, I wasn't put off completely. I chose to start over, this time choosing to vet the information I got.

Why Invest?

There is no universal reason why people choose to invest, as everyone has their own reason and purpose. For some, investing is just what you do. They have been taught that investing is the right decision to make with money, so they do it. For others, investing is a safety net for their retirement, a way to keep living comfortably even without employment income. Some invest to achieve short-term financial goals, like raising money to buy something or to use it as capital for a certain endeavor. There is no right answer when it comes to investing, but I highly recommend having a clear purpose when you embark on this journey. By pinpointing your reason for investing, you give yourself a purpose, a reason why you are investing. This, in turn, helps you focus even as you are bombarded by information about the "best" investment options. If your goal is to save up for retirement, investing in short-term investment options does not align with your goal, and investing in long-term investment options is not ideal if you are saving to make a capital purchase in five years.

Whatever your reason, investing does have its perks, with the greatest one (for me) being its ability to combat inflation. Inflation is described as the decreasing purchasing power of a currency over time, usually reflected in the rising cost of goods and services despite no changes to the quality or quantity. According to *Statista*, from February 2021 to February 2022, prices have risen by 7.9%[38], and the annual inflation in 2021 was at 4.7%, a significant increase from 2011's 3.2%. However, reported inflation is usually lower than the actual inflation, especially for the health and education industries, where expenses usually rise much faster than the reported inflation. With investment, you get the opportunity to save your money in a way that outpaces the inflation rates, essentially growing the value of your money. While some savings accounts are described as high-yield, the rate of growth is usually marginally lower than the inflation rate, essentially decreasing the value of the money saved.

Investing is not a straight line from point A to point B, as your aspirations and goals are subject to change as circumstances shift. However, it is essential that you don't quit when things get tough; instead, choose to learn and adapt to the changing tides.

Remember: The first million takes the longest, and is the hardest.

The Stock Market

Stocks, also known as shares or a company's equity, are financial investments which represent ownership in a corporation or company. Shares, essentially, give the investor claims to the company's earnings and assets. The number of shares the investor owns as a portion of the company's total outstanding shares represents their stake. Shares are issued by both private and public companies, but as the name suggests, private companies' shares are restricted to a set of specific people - usually the owners, management, and select private investors. A private company can choose to go public, in which case there will be an Initial Public Offering (IPO) where shares are made available to the public. For many private companies, the decision to go public is usually motivated by the need to raise more capital, and to give their shareholders an opportunity to reap potential gains from their investments.

Because of their ability to generate returns over a long period of time, stocks are usually considered a relatively safe investment. However, this does not mean that all stocks are safe. In addition to the companies listed on the stock exchanges, there are other shares which can be bought through the over-the-counter exchanges, also known as over-the-counter bulletin boards (OTCBB). These shares are riskier, as the listed companies are usually those that have failed to comply with the strict listing criteria of the bigger exchanges. Many of the companies listed on the OTCBB are typically small companies looking for capital to fund their operations. While there is a chance that such a company may hit its targets and result in explosive returns for its investors, this is a rarer occurrence.

Present in the stock market at every moment around the globe, across every time ozone, are millions of traders and investors, whose sentiment and actions determine the value of a company's stock. Through a stockbroker - the middleman between the buyers and sellers - shares are bought and sold every second of the day, with the laws of supply and demand dictating the price of a company's shares. In the past, stock trading had to be facilitated by human stockbrokers, which made investing largely inaccessible to many people because of the high commission fees. Apps like Ameritrade and Robinhood have revolutionized stock investment, making it easier for beginners to join the game. However, before investing in stocks, you must be clear about your goals. Generally, stock investors fall into two categories because of the two major types of stock returns:

● **Capital gains** - These are profits made when an investor sells their stock at a higher price than their purchase price. To make capital gains, the investor needs to closely monitor the market and make calculated guesses about the best time to sell so that they can make the highest gain. Essentially, this is speculation and the foundation of day trading. Investing in the stock market for the purpose of making capital gains is usually for the investors with a high tolerance for risk, unless done with a 10 year time horizon for example.

● **Dividends** - These are the share of profits that are distributed to shareholders. More conservative investors usually choose dividend investing as they get to receive relatively consistent income over longer periods of time. By investing in companies that have a long history of paying substantial dividends, the investor feels secure.

Market Cycles

Market cycles refer to the four phases observed in business environments because of the economic trends. Market cycles are driven by, and influence, investor sentiment. These cycles manifest at different times in different business environments, but the cycle is never-ending, no matter how long it takes. The cycles are only recognizable in hindsight, but the principle of speculation is based on investors aiming to predict the upcoming shifts ahead of time and curating their activities based on their calculated conclusions. Each cycle has four phases, and once one cycle ends, another starts.

● **Accumulation Phase**

This phase begins after the market has hit rock bottom. While the media is still focused on the gloom and doom of the market, early adopters and innovators start buying shares as they believe that the worst is already over. With other investors selling their shares at a loss because they held on too long, the innovators snap these up.

In this phase, the market is still bearish - **bear markets** are signified by a weak economy where there is a high supply of stocks but a weak demand, fueling price drops. However, investor sentiment during this phase is slowly shifting from negative to neutral.

• Mark-Up Phase

This phase is marked by market stability that is starting to shift upwards, with the media reports indicating that the worst is over. However, employee layoffs and unemployment are still rising at this stage. More investors have jumped on the bandwagon, and as stock prices begin to increase, greed starts to replace logic and reason. As the late investors also flock in to buy, prices keep rising, and smart investors are quick to offload their shares. Finally, as prices level off and stabilize, the more risk-averse and conservative investors also join in, causing a final upward shift (parabolic move) where investors can make the highest gains in a short period of time.

Investor sentiment shifts from neutral to bullish - **bull markets** are signified by a weak supply and great demand, resulting in higher share prices. In some cases, the market may shift from bullish to euphoric, where the markets don't reflect reality, with prices soaring as "fools" rush in.

• Distribution Phase

This phase is marked by sellers dominating the market, with investor sentiment shifting from bullish to mixed. Because of the fluctuations in stock prices, investors have periods of greed and hope interspersed with fear.

However, a negative geopolitical event or extremely bad economic news can rapidly shift investor sentiment, leading to a spiral into the mark-down phase. Investors who are not able to sell their stock at a profit settle for breaking even or even enduring a loss.

• Mark-Down Phase

For the investors still holding their positions, this is the most painful phase as the prices of their investments have fallen below what they paid for them. This phase signifies that the bottom is imminent, and for smart investors, time to start buying. The investors who buy at this phase hold on to their investments during the ensuing accumulation phase, choosing to unload their investments during the mark-up phase.

Types of Stocks

Not all stocks and shares are the same. Factors like

industry, shareholder rights, investor sentiment, earnings distribution, stock value, and economic conditions all determine how these stocks are perceived. A single stock may fall under various categories because of its inherent characteristics, and these are also subject to change over time.

Let's take a look at some of the most common types of stocks that you may come across during your investment journey:

● Common stock/Ordinary shares

Common shares are what come to mind when investment shares are mentioned. Shareholders usually have voting rights, normally capped at one share per shareholder, although some companies may have variations. Shareholders are entitled to a share of the company's earnings, in the form of dividends. In the event of liquidation, common shareholders have rights to the assets of the company, but are paid only after preferred shareholders and other debt holders have received their dues.

● Preferred stock/Preferred shares

Preferred shareholders, although they do not have any voting rights, are entitled to a regular dividend payment. They receive dividends before the common shareholders, and are repaid first if the company goes bankrupt or dissolves.

This investment method is great for conservative

investors seeking regular passive income.

● Growth stocks

These are the shares of a company that is expected to grow significantly faster than the average market growth. Any earnings accrued from these shares are usually reinvested in the company to keep facilitating its growth, profit and therefore towards a higher and more speculative stock price.

Growth stocks are usually attractive to investors looking to make capital gains as these stocks typically don't offer dividends.

● Value stocks

These are the shares of a company that seem to be priced at a range that is lower than their fundamental value because of investor sentiment. These stocks typically have low price-to-earnings (P/E) ratios and high dividend yields, but the market skepticism makes them riskier than growth stocks.

Value stocks, however, are very attractive to value investors.

● Income stocks

These are shares that pay regular dividends, which are often increasing. These investments are great for investors looking for regular income.

● Blue-chip stocks

These are shares of a large, well-established company with a great reputation and large market capitalization. These companies are usually leading within their industries, and have a successful record for generating dependable revenue. While they are usually considered to be safe investments, this is not always the case. In a bear market or black swan event, blue-chip stocks can still take a beating.

● Cyclical stocks

These are shares of companies that are directly impacted by economic trends, as they tend to perform well when the economy is thriving and people have discretionary income. When the economy weakens, these companies perform dismally, sometimes rendering the shares completely worthless. Cyclical stocks are usually those of lifestyle companies, like Netflix, Nike, etc.

This seeming predictability of the cyclical stocks' performance leads some investors to speculate and time the market, buying the stocks when they hit low values and selling them when the price increases.

● Non-cyclical stocks

These are shares of companies that are considered "recession proof" because the demand for their core products and services remains constant even during an economic downturn. These companies perform reasonably well despite the economic trends.

- Penny stocks

Penny stocks are stocks that are valued at less than $5 per share. They are usually stocks of small companies, and while some are listed on the stock exchanges, most of them trade on OTCBBs or through privately owned over-the-counter markets groups. These shares usually lack liquidity in the market because of difficulties finding the price that accurately represents the market. Because of their low liquidity, wide bid-ask spreads, and small company sizes, penny stocks are considered highly speculative.

These investments are suitable for investors who have a high tolerance for risk, and while there can be instances of explosive growth, investors are urged to have realistic expectations when putting their money in penny stocks.

Exchange-Traded Funds (ETFs)

After my initial attempt at investing, I vowed that I wouldn't get burned again because of ignorance. If I was going to lose money investing, I wouldn't regret it because I would have done my due diligence. Any loss would be because of things out of my control. I know this mentality is not really reflective of reality, but it was the only way I could jumpstart my courage. I needed the boost to make me forget my initial stupidity. I delved into stock investing, but I really couldn't decide what company or industry to focus on. The sheer abundance of options was driving me wild, and I didn't have the patience to launch a trial and error approach. So when my colleague suggested ETFs (Exchange-Traded Funds), I was intrigued. My biggest problem had a solution. Instead of choosing an item at a time, my choice was now which basket to pick.

An ETF is like a pre-arranged gift basket. Multiple securities, usually in a particular industry or with a similar theme, are pooled together. This pool is then split into shares, which are then traded on the stock exchange like a regular stock. The ETF is a great way to diversify your portfolio, as these investments include commodities, stocks, or bonds, spanning various industries or even countries.

One of the most common ETFs is the S&P 500 ETF, which tracks the performance of America's 500 largest companies, meaning that if you invest in an S&P 500 ETF, you essentially invest in 500 companies. Purchasing stock from each of these companies is costly and time-consuming, which makes the S&P ETF a convenient, low-cost, and easy way to buy a slice of the market. Three ETFs that track the S&P 500's performance include State Street Global Advisors' SPDR S&P 500 ETF (SPY), launched in January 1993, BlackRock's iShares Core S&P 500 ETF (IVV), launched in May 2000, and Vanguard's Vanguard S&P 500 ETF (VOO) launched in September 2010. There isn't much difference among these three options since returns are more or less the same - annualized at around 13.95% (11.95% when adjusted for inflation) over the past decade. Other types of ETFs include bond ETFs, commodity ETFs, currency ETFs, industry ETFs, and country ETFs, among others.

It is important to note that while ETFs, mutual funds, and index funds are all basket investments, they are not the same thing. Unlike ETFs, which can be traded at any time of the day, index funds and mutual funds are only traded at the end of the trading day. Additionally, ETFs have lower minimum investment costs compared to both index funds and mutual funds.

Investing in ETFs

While the various S&P 500 ETFs have minimal differences in terms of returns, this is not the case for the other types of ETFs. For example, investing in a Japanese or Commodity based ETF would have a wildly different ROI to the S&P 500, because it's tracking different investment vehicles and companies. Just like your stock investment, ETF investing requires that you take the time to consider your personal needs, goals, and interests before putting in your money.

- Research ETFs

There is a wide variety of ETFs to invest in, and choosing the one that will fit your needs requires you take the time to research the options that are available. Are you investing for income or growth returns? Is your investment long term or short term? Which industry or sector are you most interested in? Answering these questions will help you solidify your investment purpose, giving you a starting point.

Once your purpose is locked down, find the list of ETFs that have the potential of helping you achieve this purpose. ETFDB.com is a good starting point. Reviewing the individual ETFs, check their volume and historic returns. Does the fund have high volume or not? Funds with high volume may be easier to trade compared to low volume funds. What is the fund's expense ratio? The lower the expense ratio, the less you will pay in administrative costs. However, some funds with higher expense ratios are worth the extra cost because of the returns. Do your due diligence to avoid being hit by surprise expenses that cut into your returns. How does the fund perform? While past performance is not a sure indicator of what will happen in the future, it is still a great way to measure the viability of the fund.

- Find a trading platform

Are you more comfortable with an online broker or do you want to go for traditional broker-dealers? For most beginners, online brokerage accounts are sufficient, and apps like Robinhood have made it possible to start investing with minimal fees or at zero cost. Once you've opened your brokerage account, all you need to do is fund the account. Different brokers have different stipulations pertaining to funding the account, so confirm what you need, such as ID, etc. Many active investors usually opt for the more traditional brokerage accounts, and passive investors have the option of choosing robo-investors, although these may limit your freedom to choose which investments to focus on.

- Buy ETFs

With your brokerage account now funded, you can search for and trade the ETFs of your choosing.

If you're ready to start your investment journey, there are a few online brokers you can look into. Your choice of broker also depends on your needs and preferences, so please make sure you do your due diligence to avoid disappointments. TD Ameritrade and Fidelity Investments are both wonderful options for beginners, but if you plan on mainly using your phone, TD Ameritrade is your best bet. For ETF investing, Charles Schwab is a great option, as it has a strong ETF screening capability and makes ETF investing simple. For UK investors, Hargreaves Lansdown, IG, and Fidelity are all great options which also offer stock ISA's. If you want to access worldwide stock market exchanges, Interactive Brokers is one online broker that allows offers access to all of them within one account – from Oslo to Hong Kong.

Chapter 9 - The 3 Investing Keys – Leverage, Diversification & Dollar Cost Averaging

"Entrepreneurs should always aim to play the long game. Instant gratification cannot build a legacy."

~ Andrena Sawyer

For the first-time investor, investing can seem like a daunting task. When do I put in money? How do I know that the price is at the lowest so that I can buy? How much can I put in? Do I need to sell every time the prices increase? How much money do I need to save so that I can start investing? I was obsessed with trying to figure out the "right" amount to invest and the "right" timing. I had some money saved up by this point, but I couldn't make a move. This is not something that I alone have gone through. Many newbie investors get so overwhelmed by the thought of making the "best" choice that they end up falling for the get-rich-quick rug-pulls masquerading as "hot" investment picks. For the conservative investor with limited funds and the desire to keep investing for the long haul, **dollar cost averaging** is the best bet.

Essentially, dollar cost averaging is a simple strategy that involves depositing a set amount into your chosen investment option at regular intervals. Let's say you decide to deposit $500 or $250 every month into your chosen investment. This means that no matter the price of the investment at any given time, your investment remains the same. The market cycles do not determine your decision to invest, as this is a long-term plan. Dollar cost averaging works for the benefit of the investor because over the long term, most stocks tend to move upwards over a long enough timeframe.

Because of the constant price fluctuations, the number of shares you buy each month may fluctuate, but on average, with dollar cost averaging, your performance would be much better than if you had tried to time the market. No-load mutual funds, index funds, and ETFs are great investment options for dollar cost averaging because of the low to no fees incurred, ensuring that your contributions retain their value. Additionally, reinvesting your dividends also increases your investment, and with compound interest working for you, building wealth becomes marginally easier with this strategy.

Remember, dollar cost averaging is not for you if you're looking for short-term gains on your investment. This is an "in for the long haul" strategy for investors looking out on a long time horizon.

Leverage and your Investment

I always assumed that this was general knowledge, but when I watched *"The Hunt for the Crypto King"*, I was amazingly baffled by one of the victim's story. First, he borrowed money to invest in Bitcoin when Bitcoin underwent its euphoric cycle in 2017. When the price inevitably plummeted, he had to sell his home and, unwilling to cough up the 2% bank fee for transferring his $400k profit to his Canadian account, he put it all in a Canadian crypto exchange, and lost it all. He is not alone. As more and more investors open up about their losses, many express how they took out loans to invest. They expected returns, and a profit, so the risk seemed worth the reward. However, for many people who incur debt for investment purposes, their focus is usually on the potential benefits of the leverage. They forget that there's just as much risk of reward as there is the risk of loss.

My two cents? Don't incur leverage for investment purposes with the hopes of turning a quick profit. Take your time, use dollar cost averaging, and increase your investment contributions consistently.

Hedging

As you become more comfortable in the investment space, and your portfolio becomes larger, it becomes inevitable that you will want to find ways of diversifying your portfolio so that you can protect your investments as best as you can. No matter how stable an investment option seems at a particular point in time, there may be poor performance in the future. A long-lasting bear market is bound to put a dent in your investment, and finding ways to hedge the stock market is a great way to protect yourself. Some commodities, like gold, tend to have a stable performance despite the market trends, and sometimes the value increases even as other investment vehicles show poor performance. Silver is also a good investment commodity, although it does not hold the same power as gold. Long-term treasury bonds tend to be financially lucrative when the S&P 500 crashes, as the government buys them back in fervor and cuts prices in a bid to tamper inflation. However, treasuries in the 21st Century have had lower returns, and these returns may be even lower in the future. There are also other items that can be used to hedge the market, like artwork that is bound to appreciate in value, baseball cards, vintage cars, and Rolex watches, as well as other luxury items. However, with these luxury commodities, it is important to note that customizing a piece may lead to a value drop. Customization is usually to your personal preferences, which may not match up with the potential buyer's.

This short FYI sets up the stage for the next section of the investment journey - the high-risk speculative investment that has become so popular today.

Chapter 10 - Investing vs. Speculating (More Risky & Less Passive Strategies)

"I'd rather regret the risks that didn't work out than the chances I didn't take at all."

~ Simone Biles

It is highly unlikely that you have not heard about cryptocurrency in these current times. From Elon Musk's "to the moon" tweets and news coverage on the absurdity of Bitcoin price surges in 2020 and 2021, to Kim Kardashian and other celebrities shilling various cryptocurrencies, media and social media spaces have been overrun by cryptocurrency information. However, many people find it hard to imagine why cryptocurrencies have permeated the market with such ferocity, especially since they can't imagine what they actually do. Following its launch in 2009, Bitcoin was mostly just a token that seemed to captivate the nerds dreaming of a utopian society where citizens had a say in what the currency was worth and they could do with it as they pleased without restrictions and absurd fees.

Cryptocurrency Investing

The greatest selling point for cryptocurrency is its decentralization and trustless transactions. Because of cryptocurrency's blockchain technology, there is no reliance on a single network to store the records of transactions, which eliminates the possibility of failure if the system is hacked or tampered with. Cryptocurrency transaction records are permanent and timestamped, which eliminates reliance on third parties like banks and payment apps. Additionally, transactions cannot be completed without the crypto holder's authorization, limiting infuriating actions like payment reversals or theft. However, despite the safety and security features of cryptocurrencies, you have to remain vigilant and ensure that you are also doing your part. As a crypto owner, you have to ensure that your passwords and private keys are well guarded and safely secured. Your cryptocurrency wallet is where you store your private keys - the unique alphanumeric characters that grant you access to your cryptocurrency holdings when you want to carry out a transaction. There are two main ways of storing your wallets - hardware/cold storage and online/hot storage. Hardware/cold storage can include using backup harddisks, writing the passwords and keys on a piece of paper, or using platforms that have cold storage capabilities like Ledger, or Trezor. Because the wallet is not connected to the internet, cold storage is not susceptible to hacking, but you still

148

need to remain vigilant. You may opt for online/hot wallets, but I do not recommend this. If your wallet is compromised and your holdings stolen, there is little to no chance of recovering your losses.

What is the value of a virtual currency? If you're like me, this question has crossed your mind more than once. When I first heard about Bitcoin in 2015, I brushed it off as just another internet craze that would die out. However, as more of my favorite YouTube content creators began talking about crypto - usually stories of scams and unprecedented loss - I got curious. The value of cryptocurrency lies in its utility, which informs the behavior of investors and users. For example, Bitcoin's intended utility was to serve as a currency to aid in cross-border transactions without the restrictive red tape and bank fees. As it became more popular, investors began seeing its value as an asset. Many coins, including Bitcoin, Ethereum, and Solana, have showcased their capability for generating capital gains for investors. The more useful the coin, the more value it gains as more people are willing to invest. Another up and coming coin is Monero (XMR), and it's also one of the only truly private digital currencies. Most people wrongly assume Bitcoin is anonymous/private, when it is in fact the opposite, almost all transactions can be traced to individuals because of the requirements to provide KYC and I.D. when buying from exchanges. Please remember, if somebody knows your wallet address, they can see exactly how much bitcoin or other coins you have, so please be vigilant – you wouldn't want everybody in the world to know how much is in your bank account, regardless of whether you have $100 Million or $0.

However, some cryptocurrencies are created with no particular utility in mind. Meme/joke coins like Shibu Inu and Dogecoin were created for fun, and their meteoric rise shocked even their creators. With over 15,000 cryptocurrency coins in the market, it figures that not all of them hold much value since their utility and demand are almost-nonexistent. Many of the people who bought into Dogecoin after Elon Musk's iconic tweet were left holding the bag, some incurring massive losses that saw them lose their entire life savings. In a nutshell, this is the level of risk present when investing in the crypto space. In January 2022, cryptocurrency prices recently plummeted following China banning cryptocurrency mining and trading.

If you're risk-averse, cryptocurrency investment is definitely not your cup of tea. But for the robust at heart who want to try their hand in the virtual asset space, here's what you need to keep in mind as you begin your journey:

- **Choosing a Cryptocurrency Exchange**

Just like traditional investing, you need to choose a

platform to trade your tokens. Your choice may vary depending on your needs, the exchange's fees, and coin options you need, as well as other services the exchange may be providing, such as wallet storage and exchange-specific utility tokens, to give more perks when using the site.

Currently, the most popular exchanges include Coinbase, Kraken, Binance, Gemini, Kucoin, and Bitfinex, among others. Alternatively, you may choose to trade through traditional brokers who offer cryptocurrency services. Before committing to any specific exchange, make sure you perform the appropriate research to find out whether your needs will be met.

- **Trading**

If you decide to sign up with a know-your-customer (KYC) platform, you will need personal identification documents to trade on the site. However, with just your bank account information and a secure internet connection, you are ready to start trading. Buying an entire unit of a cryptocurrency may be expensive, but this is made cheaper and affordable through purchasing fractions of the coin.

As long as you have enough funds, you can purchase the cryptocurrencies as you please. However, ensure that your private keys are stored securely to avoid loss. Depending on your needs and the market trends, you are free to trade as you please. However, please remember that the profit you make from selling your holdings is subject to capital gains tax, so plan accordingly to avoid surprises from the IRS.

However, it is worth noting here that investing in the cryptocurrency market is not limited to tokens. You may choose to invest in crypto company mining stocks, blockchain based ETFs, crypto funds, or crypto futures.

The Metaverse

How does one invest in the metaverse? Is what you're probably thinking. As technology evolves and grows, there are endless new opportunities for early adopters, and risk in spades! Back in October 2021, Mark Zuckerberg (otherwise known as Zucks) announced Facebook's foray into the virtual space with its own metaverse, and the company rebranded to Meta. While virtual universes have been in existence for a while - think Minecraft and Roblox - Zuckerberg's dream is to have the virtual connection between people enhanced in a more interactive way. Non-fungible tokens (NFTs), crypto coins, and virtual real estate are the main investment options that exist in these universes, giving investors the opportunity to make capital gains upon the sale of their investments when they appreciate in value.

For example, Axie Infinity's (AXS) play-to-earn allows its gamers to collect the AXS coin, and with the coin's increased value following the announcement of the Axie Infinity: Origin upgrade, investors are set to make a profit when the demand for coins exceeds supply. In December 2021, Snoop Dogg purchased land in Sandbox to create Snoopverse. He's since sold passes to have fans enjoy perks like new NFTs, early access to play-to-earn games, and tours of the universe being created. For Snoop Dogg, investing in the virtual world provides new platforms for him to connect with his fans and offer more fanservice.

Because the space is relatively new, investing in the metaverse is a highly speculative option, and is not for everyone. Decentraland, Sandbox, Epik Prime, and games such as Roblox are popular at the moment, but others, such as Star Atlas, while still in development, are showing great potential for future gains. Before investing in the metaverse, make sure you have all the relevant information you need.

Remember: Do not invest what you're not willing to go to 0.

Non-Fungible Tokens (NFTs)

From hits like CryptoPunks and Bored Ape Yacht Club to flops like many of the others, and outright rug pulls like Frosties, Baller Ape Club and Evolved Apes, NFT investment is a high risk endeavor that requires a high tolerance for risk. Built on blockchain technology, NFTs are digital assets that represent both tangible and intangible items. The NFTs unique address, its built-in authentication, is the proof of ownership, setting it apart from digital copies of the same. Essentially, there is no limit to what can be turned into an NFT, but its value differs depending on the NFT creator, the demand, and its utility.

The NFT space has given artists, creators, celebrities, influencers, companies, and others the chance to monetize their work. While there are some people using plagiarized work to create NFTs, such projects are usually quickly shunned when the owners of the work speak out. Investing in NFTs, like Pudgy Penguins or BAYC (Bored Ape Yacht Club), is highly speculative and requires vigilance and tremendous research. Rug pulls and scams are prevalent in the NFT space, but there are some NFTs that are worth their investment because of the amount investors are willing to pay. Tom Brady bought a Bored Ape Yacht Club NFT for $430,000, and the cheapest Bored Ape on OpenSea is about $400,000. Note, however, these are priced in Ethereum as opposed to dollars. Some celebrities are using NFTs for the utility, like EDM's 3LAU (Justin Blau), who issued limited NFTs for his album's third year anniversary. Holders of the NFTs were granted access to new versions of the album's original songs, original album works, and access to never-before-heard music on his website. Some also received physical items like records.

The utility of an NFT can give it a tremendous value, making it a great investment opportunity when resold. Do your due diligence before investing in any NFT, and remember that the market's high volatility makes the NFT a risky investment.

Investing in the highly speculative digital asset market can be rewarding, but the risks can outweigh the potential gains. For this reason, these investments should not be the foundation of your investment strategy. Instead, *weight* your investments properly, prioritizing the lower and medium risk investments. The riskier investments should be at the tip of the investment pyramid to limit the losses incurred in case of poor market performance. In my opinion, your riskier investments should not make up more than 10% of your entire investment portfolio. This way, you are able to control the bleeding when losses are incurred. On the other hand, with one of these smaller, more speculative investments - it's certainly possible to have a 10x or 100x gain within a short space of time.

Single Stock Investments

Unlike ETFs, (baskets of stocks grouped together into a single fund), choosing single stocks to invest in is a time-consuming process that requires constant monitoring and decision making depending on your investment goals. With single stock investments, your returns are wholly dependent on the company's performance and market sentiment.

Before choosing the stock(s) you want to invest in, figure out your purpose for investing - are you looking for consistent dividend income or capital gains? Are you banking on the company's growth or do you want well established companies with consistent dividend payouts? What's your risk tolerance? How long do you plan on holding the stock? Do you have the time to monitor the stock's performance to guide your future decisions? There are thousands of stocks to choose from, and even if you wanted to, you could never go through each of the companies' income statements to figure out which one is the best one for you. Because of this, choosing stocks based on your end goals helps you narrow down your options.

Which industry are you interested in? *Energy? Precious Metals? Shipping? Retail?* What's the industry's recent performance and future outlook? Are individual stocks the best bet for this industry?

Some market factors drive the performance of industries, with pharmaceutical companies hitting record highs when there's a new drug hitting the market, or during a health crisis like the COVID-19 plandemic. Technology companies perform well when there's new innovation within the industry, which makes investing in tech companies a great option for a growth investor. This helps you whittle down the companies further. By looking at the general performance of companies over the years, you get to find the ones that will best mesh with your needs. Is the company overvalued or undervalued? The price-to-earnings ratio (P/E ratio) is one way to determine this. For growth investors, an undervalued company is a good bet because of the speculated growth and capital gains to be obtained. However, it is important to determine why the company is undervalued or overvalued.

After selecting a stock to invest in, as an investor, you need to remain vigilant and monitor how the markets, and the company in particular, is performing. The prices of stock, depending on the industry, fluctuate for various reasons. For example, news of a hack is problematic for a tech company, and will affect the stock prices. Additionally, government regulation, bad press, criminal activities, and general market trends all influence the price of the stock. Unlike ETFs, which may have a few stable stocks in the basket balancing the more volatile ones, single stocks mean that you will bear the full consequence of the stock's performance.

When investing in single stocks, always ensure that your investments are diversified enough to prevent total destruction in case of poor performance. A good rule of thumb is to never invest more than 7% of your portfolio in a single stock. Of course, you could get lucky going all-in one stock, but this would require immense conviction and understanding of the markets.

Also, beware of buying too many stocks that rely on speculation/growth, and get some *value stocks* in there too.

Real Estate Investment: Single vs. Multi-Family

Homeownership is part of the American Dream, as we have all dreamt of having our own homes. Buying a home is a celebrated feat, a milestone that the current market is pushing further and further out of our reach. For many people, investing in real estate is the ultimate goal since it is considered a more stable investment strategy. Property values tend to increase, and there are various tax advantages associated with property investment. However, getting into the game as a beginner can be risky, especially if you fail to do your due diligence.

Investing in real estate, compared to other investments, requires a pretty solid credit score. If you're buckling under the pressure of debt, it is not the right time to enter the real estate market. Securing a mortgage with a poor credit score is near impossible, and if a lender agrees to lend you the money, you're probably going to get stuck with absurd interest rates and underwritings. Real estate investment is primarily about the income generated by the property, but you could also enter the game with the plan of making capital gains from selling the property. Investing in rental property may involve investing in single-family homes, or multi-family homes. A single-family home is much easier to maintain and may come with a smaller price tag, but the income generated from the property may translate to minimal profits. Additionally, with single-family homes, hiring help to perform repairs may rack up costs that cut into your profits. A single-family property investment is akin to putting all your eggs in one basket, as you would have 100% vacancy rate if your tenants decide to move out. And if they are unwilling to pay or pay their rent late, this impacts your mortgage payment immediately. Single family homes are an active investment, so you need to be prepared to handle all issues that arise yourself.

Multi-family real estate investment has numerous perks and drawbacks. Securing financing for property investment is much harder, as there are stringent requirements to be met. Unlike the mortgage on your home, you will be required to put up a higher down payment - ranging from 15% to 20%. You also need to have enough savings to cover at least two to three months of the costs associated with the financing. Fortunately, with multi-family property, your income is higher, and unless all tenants move out at the same time, you are assured of income that will cover the maintenance costs of the home as you screen new tenants. Because the income is higher, you can also afford to hire an agency to handle the maintenance of the property, allowing you to be more passive in the day-to-day operations.

However, as a beginner, do not be tricked into buying a rundown property with the promise of turning a profit later. If you are not familiar with the industry, the cost of fixing up a property will consume you, leaving you frustrated or worse, in tremendous debt and with no income. When selecting a property, choose a state with low property taxes, and areas that are close to necessary amenities like shops, restaurants, schools, etc. Up and coming neighborhoods with low crime rates are also great investment options.

If you're looking for less involvement in the process, real estate investment trusts (REITs) are good investment opportunities. Real estate investment trusts (REITs) are companies that invest in property for the long term, holding massive portfolios that investors buy into. REITs are great investment options for investors looking to earn an income from their investment, as these companies are required to pay out at least 90% of their net income to investors. VNQ is one of the most popular real estate REITs that purchases hotels, offices and other kinds of real estate.

Property investment, like any other investment option, should not be embarked on without performing due diligence. Because of the associated tax benefits, - write-offs include management fees, insurance, fees incurred when screening tenants, mortgage payments, depreciation, etc. - property investment is a great long-term investment when done right. The capital gains when you decide to sell the property are also a great benefit. If you have the risk appetite to take on 'good debt,' meet the required criteria, and are interested in a long-term but worthy investment, real estate is a great venture to engage in.

Investing, in general, has always seemed out of reach for Black women. With the challenges we face when trying to amass wealth, we find it difficult to even discuss matters relating to wealth and investing, believing that it is out of our reach. News segments and forums discussing wealth and investments predominantly feature white men, with the rare Black man lending their voice to the arguments. But Black women and people of color? They are rarely the faces we imagine when we need financial advice. Despite this, there are Black women who have made their mark in the investment space, showing up and winning. Melissa Bradley, the managing director of 1863 Ventures, founded the company to help entrepreneurs of color access the funding they were unable to secure. Arlan Hamilton, the founder and managing partner of Backstage Capital, has dedicated her company to minimizing the funding disparities in tech by backing entrepreneurs of color, women, and/or LGBT[39]. More Black women are also willing to discuss their investment, with Black "finfluencers" (financial influencers) using their voices to offer sound advice about the various investment opportunities and tools available for us. Toni Tone of 1xtra's *Money Moves,* financial coach Bola Sol, Kia Commodore's podcast *Pennies to Pounds,* and Patricia Bright's *The Break*, are just some of the financial channels that give Black women the information they need to take the first step into the world of investing[40].

Chapter 11 - Your Goal & Strategy

"Girls and women of our race must not be afraid to take hold of business endeavor and, by patient industry, close economy, determined effort, and close application to business, wring success out of a number of business opportunities that lie at their doors."

~ Madam CJ Walker

Financial independence, at its core, is subjective. $1,500 a month in discretionary income is more than enough for some people, but for others, $10,000 is barely enough to cover their basic lifestyle expenses. When I started planning my finances, I had the Suburbia McMansion dream, designer labels, fancy nights out, and an Instagram feed filled with vacations and spa days. As I made it to the other side of 30, all I wanted was enough money to pay for multiple subscription services, $30 bottles of wine, fancy matching pajamas, and an immersive sound system. The McMansion now scares me, so I dream of a nice cottage in a semi-rural area, and a big enough compound to hold a couple of chicken coops and a veggie garden. I love being cozy, and the jet-setting lifestyle is not for me.

My mother, on the other hand, is quick to fly out when she has enough money. She has always wanted a big home, but I had to make her choose between property taxes and vacations. It was a no-brainer for her. I have friends who spend an absurd amount of money on things I consider trivial, but since they are not incurring debt to afford them, I have no qualms. Our financial needs are as diverse as we are, and our spending habits differ immensely. As you embark on your journey to financial freedom, what are your goals? What is your income goal per month? How much in passive income are you aiming for? How does your dream lifestyle look? What are the costs of maintaining this lifestyle while still hitting your savings and investment goals? Do you have a target number?

Whatever your lifestyle, income, or investment goals may be, the first step is to make your way out of debt. From a negative financial level to the ground level, where your most pressing debt has been cleared. Then the next step is to make it up the stairs, one step at a time. Figure out how to keep your expenses low, and at the same time, find ways to increase your income. Save enough to cover your expenses for a few months, then focus on investing your money to build up your portfolio. Remember that this path is not linear, and there will be moments where you falter or make decisions that threaten to destroy your progress. No matter what, don't give up. Keep fighting, and pick yourself up every single time, no matter how bleak things may seem.

The first million is the hardest.

F. I. R. E. Movement

Financial Independence, Retire Early (F.I.R.E) is an online financial management movement that focuses on aggressive saving and investment. Essentially, FIRE is about cutting down on expenses as much as possible, and maximizing your income. The difference is saved and invested with the goal of slowing down or retiring early.

Some adopt the FIRE strategy, not for the goal of early retirement, but to achieve financial independence. They are looking to live life on their terms, not shackled down by the demands of their career, especially if they are looking for time to explore more fulfilling activities, or passion projects. For them, FIRE is the vehicle that gets them to focus on being fulfilled, rather than just making a living and spending everything on activities that distract them from life's problems and their own unfulfillment. For others, FIRE is about early retirement. About leaving the workforce, either partially or permanently, while they have the energy to pursue their hobbies and activities that keep them content. The practitioners of FIRE generally fall under these categories;

- Fat FIRE - Their goal is to earn more and save more while still maintaining the current lifestyle. Essentially, they live as they have been living, and focus on making more so that they can save more. This strategy means that they will take longer to achieve their saving goals, and they may hit snags when their income increase is not substantial fast enough.

- Lean FIRE - This is what most people assume FIRE is all about. This strategy is the most aggressive, as it usually incorporates drastically cutting down expenses, and living with only the bare minimum to maximize savings and investments. Minimalism is commonly adopted in Lean FIRE, and the practitioners decry materialistic pursuits.

Because of the drastic lifestyle changes and adopted practices, Lean FIRE is usually the hardest to adopt for most people.

- Barista FIRE - This is for people who are not really looking to fully retire, but rather, find a way to pursue their dreams without being held back by their jobs and financial obligations. For these people, they may save as aggressively as the Lean FIRE practitioners, but once they have attained their goal, they slow down. Instead of getting stuck in their jobs, they choose to pursue passion projects or part-time work to keep earning money for living expenses, and to qualify for benefits.

They may quit their part-time job and travel, but pick up work on the way just to keep from dipping too much into their savings and emergency funds.

For me, Barista FIRE has been the ultimate goal. While I am not really a participant in the FIRE movement, I do adopt a few of the strategies to help me achieve my financial goals. For example, I ascribe to the practice of tracking down my expenses so that I can figure out what I need to cut out, and what doesn't serve my financial goals. I've also been slowly letting go of my attachment to material items in a bid to raise my savings. It gets difficult, but the months where I reach my targets are the most fulfilling.

So, how much is enough to retire? Only you can answer that question. While many put the number at $1,000,000, this doesn't take into account individual needs and desires. Also, what happens if a chunk of your funds are taken up by an emergency expense? The most popular calculation is 25x your annual expenses, factoring in inflation. This calculation also bases the number on an average withdrawal of 4% annually for living expenses. You may choose to follow this system, but there is no right answer. The only advice I have is this - **No matter what, don't give up!**

Chapter 12 – The Power of Repetition

"You can't just sit there and wait for people to give you that golden dream. You've got to get out there and make it happen for yourself."

~ Diana Ross

If you've ever tried to develop a new habit, you know how hard it is not to revert to your old, comfortable ways. For many people who are trying to get out of debt, the discomfort of not having what you want is sometimes enough to spark a sequence of decisions that snowball out of control. They end up worse off than before, and it seems even more impossible to crawl out of the now bigger hole. Your journey to financial freedom will test your patience, make you uncomfortable, and have you questioning your goals, dreams, and desires. Is this really worth it? How long is this going to last? What am I getting out of this? Interspersed with these moments of despair will be moments of glory when you hit your targets. The little wins will feel massive, the fuel that will keep you moving towards your goal.

That's why I recommend setting up a reward system for yourself and/or your family. When you win, don't start catastrophizing and wondering how it may all go wrong. Rather, lean into the joy of the accomplishment. Find an activity or anything you enjoy and indulge in. However, be sure that your reward will not negatively impact your progress. For example, go out to a nice restaurant, take a day off to have a round of golf - or go to the football game and get a little crazy.

As with many things in life, my go-to piece of advice is - **stay consistent.** Consistently working towards achieving your dreams, even if you are taking the tiniest of steps, is better than waiting for the moment where you can sprint to the goal. The beauty of consistency is that it gets you to build the habit, so that when you find yourself making greater strides, you automatically know what you are supposed to do, and what to expect from yourself. The only difference is the magnitude of the input and expected output. Consistency calls for you to persevere through the times when you don't think you can make any progress. It calls for you to choose your goals over your immediate comfort, to fight the urge to revert back to your old ways, and come out from the other side stronger than before.

And, when/if your hard work and consistency pay off, it's only right to empower others. As Black women, we need to make sure that our daughters, sisters, and mothers also get the much-needed help so that they can also escape the financial pitfalls that are keeping us locked in financial distress. Your impact doesn't have to be big. Start with your small circle. Pull others up with you. Show them why it's worth the effort. Extending a helping hand takes nothing from us. Rather, it gives us the chance to start a movement that will help our community lift itself up from the clutches of financial disadvantage.

As former First Lady Michelle Obama said: *"You may not always have a comfortable life. And you will not always be able to solve all the world's problems all at once. But don't ever underestimate the impact you can have because history has shown us that courage can be contagious, and hope can take on a life of its own."*

Conclusion

Black women, and the Black community as a whole, have been held back for generations, left to fight tooth and nail just to attain the basic tools to survive. As we were busy finding footing and any little food we could to place on the table, the table was pushed a little further away. For our great grandparents and grandparents, the way out for the children was the education system. I grew up with the message being drummed into me. Unless I was really talented in sports or musically inclined, which I was not, education was the only way out of the trenches. Many of the people I know were fed the same message. But, the education system is broken, and rigged against us. Resources are scarce, and our teachers are too overwhelmed to explain how the real world works. We were never once taught about financial freedom in school.

But, despite all the odds stacked against us, Black women are rallying up and fighting back. We are looking for ways to help our fellow underrepresented comrades, with Black women now finding ways to educate their fellow sisters, or fighting the system to make sure that said sisters are represented in the market. The hair and beauty industry is a testament to how far we have come as a community. The financial sector, although slower to adapt, is also a space where more and more Black women have set up camp, with Black women pushing for high paying jobs, and investing in companies and investment opportunities that we once overlooked, or weren't even told about.

This book is part of my contribution to the community, to the Black women who are looking for a way to thrive, not just survive. Financial independence is something we all deserve, but unfortunately, the world is not as generous as we'd all wish it to be. By highlighting the path I took to reach a point where I could sleep at night without breaking out in cold sweat because of the looming financial disaster that was plaguing my days, I hope that my readers will see that it's not as bleak as it may seem. Financial freedom is a culmination of three things - debt eradication, income maximization (coupled with expense minimization), and investing. By eliminating liability, you get the chance to focus on creating wealth. Being rich is not enough - we have to create wealth, not only for our own family's benefits, but to give our community the boost it desperately needs. If our children start with even slightly better odds than we did, it is worth the pains, trials, and tribulations of a few foregone luxuries.

Getting out of debt is perhaps the hardest step, as it calls for us to make a difficult choice - sacrifice the comforts of now for a brighter future. It requires us to do all we can, banking on our reservoirs of faith and hope, to lessen the burden we have. Once we have dug ourselves out of the trenches, we are still far away from the goal post. Income generation is more than just the pay stub we carry home. It is about making money that will last us a lifetime, and beyond, into generational wealth. Investment vehicles are designed to complement our salaries, but what if we are not making enough? The advent of side hustles, utilizing our skills and talent for our own benefits, has given us an alternative path to income maximization. For some, this involves getting a promotion, a second job or contractual work, but for others, this involves banking on their innovation and creativity to carve out a market niche. No matter what it is, maximizing your income will require commitment, dedication, and unwavering faith in your ability to fight for your own success. Even as you increase your income, you still need to watch out for *lifestyle creep*, and adopt conscious spending habits that will keep your goals within reach.

With this book, I have shown you the options available to you as you embark on your financial independence journey. These strategies work, and I hope that you will, at least, create a strategy that will resonate with your life, circumstances, and goals, and propel you to make changes to reflect the life that you want to live.

Thank you so much for reading this book. I appreciate you for making it this far. If you loved the book, please consider leaving a glowing 5* review on Amazon or Audible. I would love to hear from you (follow me on twitter @BrandyBrooksAuthor), and I appreciate all the support you extend outwards.

I wish you all the very best in your journey to financial freedom.

Sincerely, Brandy Brooks

Additional Resources:

Your journey to financial freedom will require further skills and knowledge, and if you are looking for more tools and resources to help you along the way, here are some of the financial books and coaches that have played a great part in my own journey.

- Books

The Richest Man in Babylon by George Samuel Clason

Atomic Habits by James Clear

The Millionaire Next Door by Thomas J. Stanley

Financial Peace by Dave Ramsey

Way of the Turtle by Curtis M. Faith

Zero Debt by Lynette Khalfani-Cox

Clever Girl Finance by Bola Sokunbi

- Podcasts

Journey to Launch by Jamila Souffrant

Bad with Money by Gaby Dunn

Brown Ambition by Madi Woodruff and Tiffany Aliche

Redefining Wealth by Patrice Washington

The Money Guy Show by Brian Preston

The Financial Grownup by Bobbi Rebell

Side Hustle Pro by Nicaula Matthews Okome

Clever GIrls Know by Bola Sokunbi

These are not even remotely exhaustive, but they are the ones that have had the most impact on my financial journey, and I am always grateful for their impact on my life and learning experience.

References

1.   History.com Editors. (2022, February 9). *Black History Milestones: Timeline*. HISTORY. https://www.history.com/topics/black-history/black-history-milestones

2.   Wilkerson, I. (2020). *Caste (Oprah's Book Club): The Origins of Our Discontents* (Reprint ed.). Random House.

3.   Burke, L. (n.d.). *Housing Redlining and Its Lingering Effects on Education Opportunity*. The Heritage Foundation. Retrieved April 20, 2022, from https://www.heritage.org/education/report/housing-redlining-and-its-lingering-effects-education-opportunity

4.   *African Americans - African American life during the Great Depression and the New Deal*. (n.d.). Encyclopedia Britannica. Retrieved April 20, 2022, from https://www.britannica.com/topic/African-American/African-American-life-during-the-Great-Depression-and-the-New-Deal

5. Gerstein, J. (2021, February 17). *A Black couple's home value skyrocketed after a white woman pretended to be the homeowner during an appraisal*. Insider. https://www.insider.com/black-couple-lowballed-on-home-price-because-of-race-2021-2

6. Scott, T., Lake, Z., Redman, M., Brown, J., Nunes, A., & Effron, L. (2020, October 15). *Couple says they faced discrimination in home appraisal because of wife's race*. ABC News. https://abcnews.go.com/US/couple-faced-discrimination-home-appraisal-wifes-race/story?id=73203432

7. Schultz, K. (2017, March 25). *Tanya McDowell is out of the shadows and living with no regrets*. The Hour. https://www.thehour.com/news/article/Tanya-McDowell-is-out-of-the-shadows-and-living-11027917.php

8. Sharif, D. (2019, September 14). *Felicity Huffman Gets 2 Weeks in Jail for Gaming Educational System — Not So Long Ago, a Black Mom Wasn't So L*. The Root. https://www.theroot.com/felicity-huffman-gets-2-weeks-in-jail-for-gaming-educat-1838111418

9. Campbell, A. F. (2018, April 18). *Dreadlocks Lawsuit: A black woman who lost a job offer because she refused to cut her dreadlocks*

is asking th. . . . Vox. https://www.vox.com/2018/4/18/17242788/chastity-jones-dreadlock-job-discrimination

10. Schwartztol, L. (2015, April 26). *Predatory Lending: Wall Street Profited, Minority Families Paid the Price*. American Civil Liberties Union. https://www.aclu.org/blog/racial-justice/race-and-economic-justice/predatory-lending-wall-street-profited-minority

11. Branch, M. M. (n.d.). *Maggie Lena Walker (1864–1934) – Encyclopedia Virginia*. Encyclopediavirginia.Org. Retrieved April 20, 2022, from https://encyclopediavirginia.org/entries/walker-maggie-lena-1864-1934/

12. *vieilles*. (n.d.). Flickr.Com. Retrieved April 20, 2022, from https://www.flickr.com/photos/vieilles_annonces/3639763251

13. Connley, C. (2020, November 6). *How Stacey Abrams, LaTosha Brown and other Black women changed the course of the 2020 election*. CNBC. https://www.cnbc.com/2020/11/06/black-women-continue-to-be-the-democratic-partys-most-powerful-weapon.html

14. Madani, D. (2022, February 13). *Erin Jackson brings home gold, first Black woman to*

win speed skating medal at the Winter Olympics.
NBC News.
https://www.nbcnews.com/news/olympics/erin-jackson-brings-home-gold-first-black-woman-win-speed-skating-meda-rcna16042

15. Jones, M. (2021, August 17). *Simone Manuel: first Black female swimmer to win individual Olympic gold*. United States Olympic & Paralympic Museum. https://usopm.org/simone-manuel-became-the-first-black-female-swimmer-to-win-individual-olympic-gold/

16. Ray, S. (2021, July 9). *14-Year-Old Girl From Louisiana Becomes First African-American To Win National Spelling Bee*. Forbes. https://www.forbes.com/sites/siladityaray/2021/07/09/14-year-old-girl-from-louisiana-becomes-first-african-american-to-win-national-spelling-bee/?sh=4a55d8ff308d

17. *Althea Gibson | Biography, Titles, & Facts*. (n.d.). Encyclopedia Britannica. Retrieved April 20, 2022, from https://www.britannica.com/biography/Althea-Gibson

18. *Oprah on Why Your Mind Defines Your Life*. (2000, September 15). Oprah.Com. https://www.oprah.com/spirit/oprah-on-why-your-mind-defines-your-life

19. Bridges, F. (2018, November 25). *Michelle Obama's Advice To Young People In Her New Book, "Becoming."* Forbes. https://www.forbes.com/sites/francesbridges/2018/11/18/michelle-obamas-message-to-young-people-in-her-new-book-becoming/

20. Ranasinghe, D. (2021, September 14). *Global debt is fast approaching record $300 trillion - IIF*. Reuters. https://www.reuters.com/business/global-debt-is-fast-approaching-record-300-trillion-iif-2021-09-14/

21. *U.S. National Debt Clock : Real Time*. (n.d.). Www.Usdebtclock.Org. Retrieved April 20, 2022, from https://www.usdebtclock.org/

22. *Household Debt and Credit Report - FEDERAL RESERVE BANK of NEW YORK*. (n.d.). Www.Newyorkfed.Org. Retrieved April 20, 2022, from https://www.newyorkfed.org/microeconomics/hhdc.html

23. NerdWallet. (n.d.). *NerdWallet's 2021 American Household Credit Card Debt Study*. Retrieved April 20, 2022, from https://www.nerdwallet.com/blog/average-credit-card-debt-household/

24. Hanson, M. (2022, April 11). *Student Loan Debt Statistics*. Education Data Initiative. https://educationdata.org/student-loan-debt-statistics

25. Yearwood, L. T. (2019, September 6). *Many minorities avoid seeking credit due to generations of discrimination. Why that keeps them back*. CNBC. https://www.cnbc.com/2019/09/01/many-minorities-avoid-seeking-credit-due-to-decades-of-discrimination.html

26. Singletary, M. (2020, October 16). *Credit scores are supposed to be race-neutral. That's impossible*. Www.Washingtonpost.Com. https://www.washingtonpost.com/business/2020/10/16/how-race-affects-your-credit-score/

27. *Good Debt vs. Bad Debt - Types of Good and Bad Debts*. (2021, May 5). Debt.Org. https://www.debt.org/advice/good-vs-bad/

28. Berman, J. (2021, November 13). *'I can't imagine the day when I'm not paying.' Black women are being crushed by the student debt crisis — and demanding action*. MarketWatch. https://www.marketwatch.com/story/i-cant-imagine-the-day-when-im-not-paying-black-women-are-being-crushed-by-the-student-debt-crisis-and-demanding-action-11635948623

29. Alvarez, J. (2020, July 20). *Good debt vs. bad debt: Why what you've been told is probably wrong*. CNBC. https://www.cnbc.com/2020/07/20/good-debt-vs-bad-debt-why-what-youve-been-told-is-probably-wrong.html

30. The Daily Beast. (2017, April 25). *Median Wealth for Single Black Women: $5*. https://www.thedailybeast.com/cheats/2010/03/10/median-wealth-for-single-black-women-5

31. Chauncey Alcorn, CNN Business. (2021, June 18). *3.5 million Black American households have a negative net worth, new study finds*. CNN. https://edition.cnn.com/2021/06/18/business/black-wealth-mckinsey-study/index.html

32. *Living On $650K A Year In Los Angeles | Millennial Money*. (2022, February 28). [Video]. YouTube. https://www.youtube.com/watch?v=FHyRVMOCLOA&t=18s&ab_channel=CNBCMakeIt

33. *Living On $175K A Year In NYC & Georgia | Millennial Money*. (2021, January 7). [Video]. YouTube. https://www.youtube.com/watch?v=aPqte8BNJYc&t=29s&ab_channel=CNBCMakeIt

34. *How I Made Over $725,000 Designing Luxury Bags While Earning An MBA | On The*

Side. (2022, January 6). [Video]. YouTube. https://www.youtube.com/watch?v=K2Q0cpUP37 A&t=51s&ab_channel=CNBCMakeIt

35. *LeanIn.Org| poll: Equal pay day 2021*. (n.d.). SurveyMonkey. Retrieved April 20, 2022, from https://www.surveymonkey.com/curiosity/lean-in-poll-equal-pay-day-2021/

36. Reporter, G. S. (2022, February 12). *Black women say goodbye to the job and hello to their own businesses*. The Guardian. https://www.theguardian.com/business/2022/feb/1 2/black-women-say-goodbye-to-the-job-and-hello-to-their-own-businesses

37. *Black Women Are More Likely to Start a Business than White Men*. (2021, May 11). Harvard Business Review. https://hbr.org/2021/05/black-women-are-more-likely-to-start-a-business-than-white-men

38. Statista. (2022, March 14). *United States - monthly inflation rate in February 2022*. https://www.statista.com/statistics/273418/unadjus ted-monthly-inflation-rate-in-the-us/#:%7E:text=The%20annual%20inflation%20rat e%20in,has%20weakened%20in%20recent%20ye ars

39. *Meet 10 Kickass Black Female Venture Capitalists You Should Know*. (n.d.). The Founder Institute. Retrieved April 20, 2022, from https://fi.co/insight/ten-black-female-venture-capitalists-you-should-know

40. Thomas-Bailey, C. (2021, May 4). *Money Moves: How Black Women Are Finding The Joy In Investing*. Refinery29. https://www.refinery29.com/en-gb/black-women-investing-money-pandemic